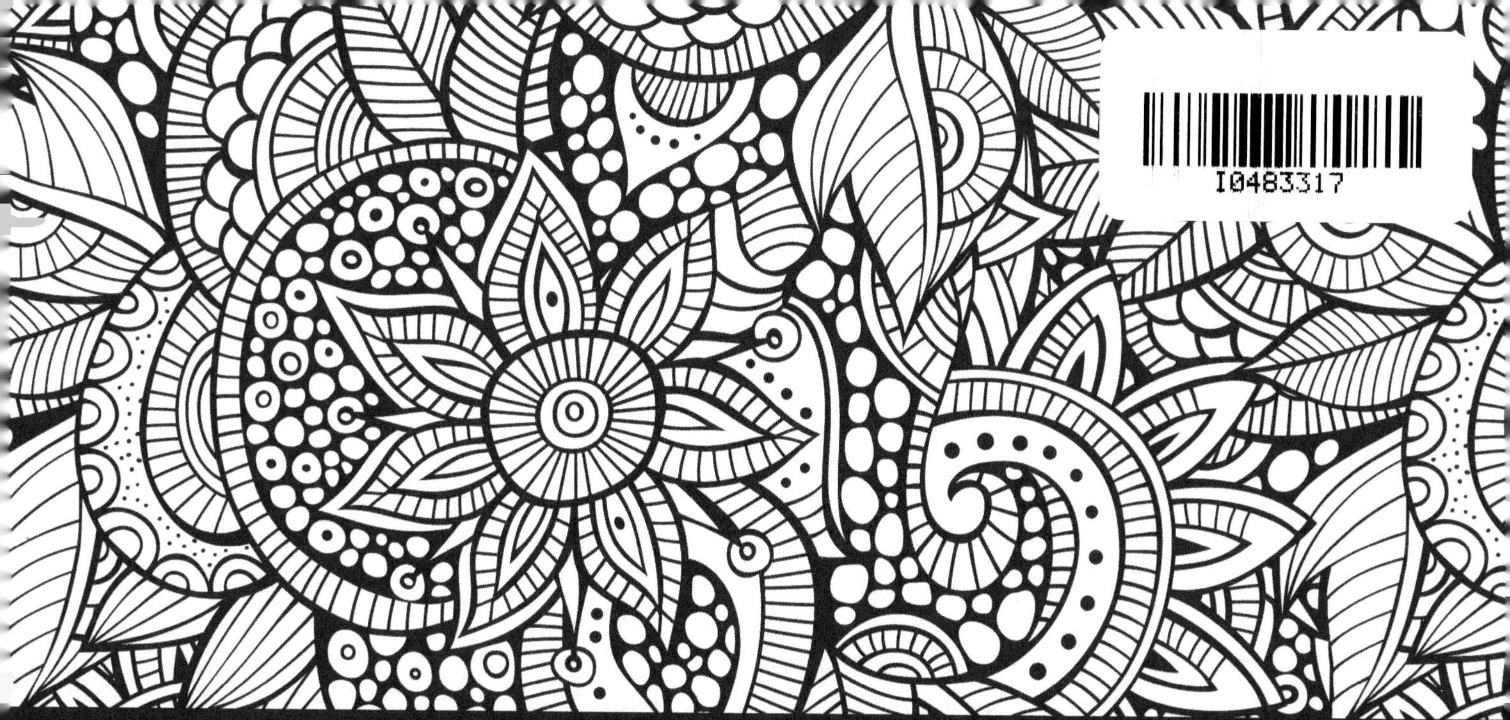

# ❧ SWIRLS ❧
## COLORING BOOK
## RELAXING DESIGNS

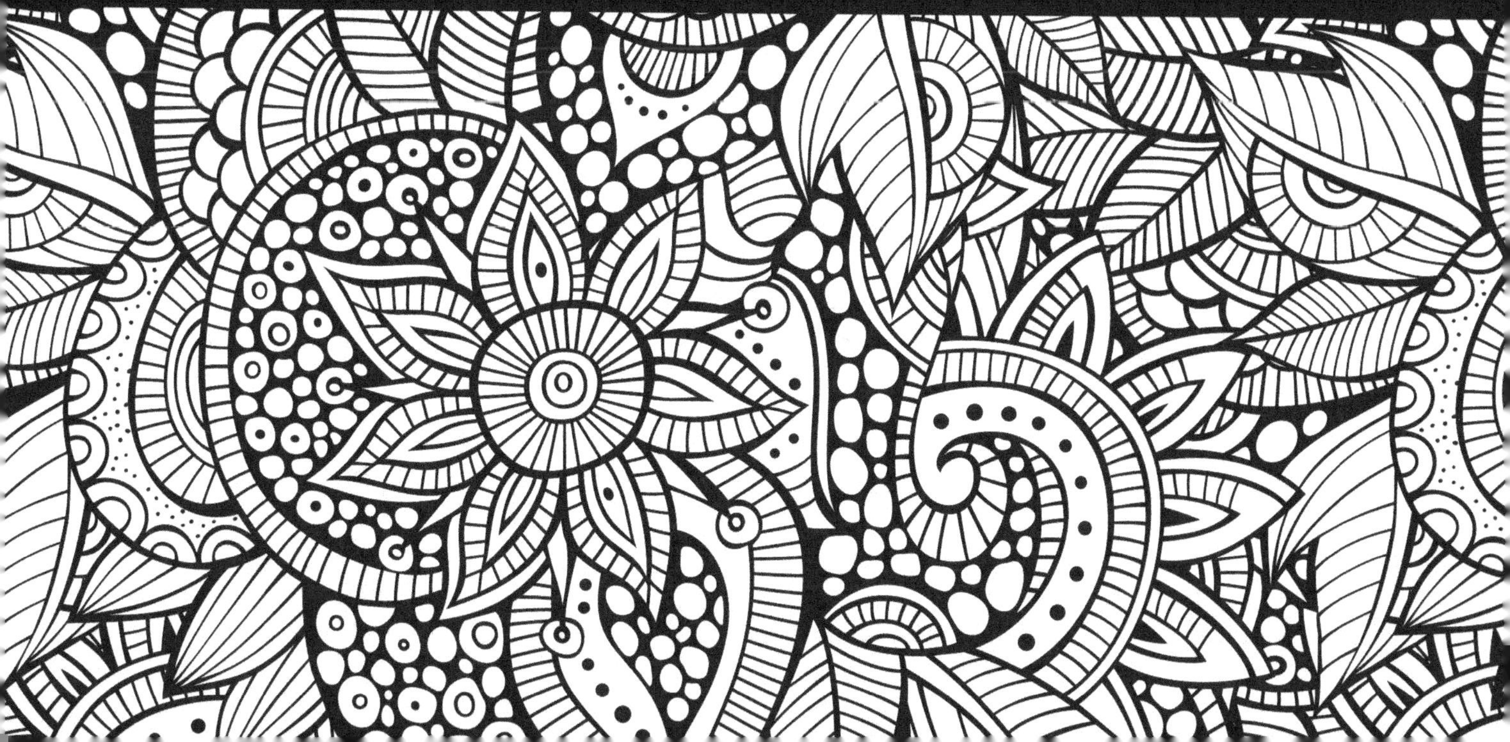

# Preview of Coloring Pages

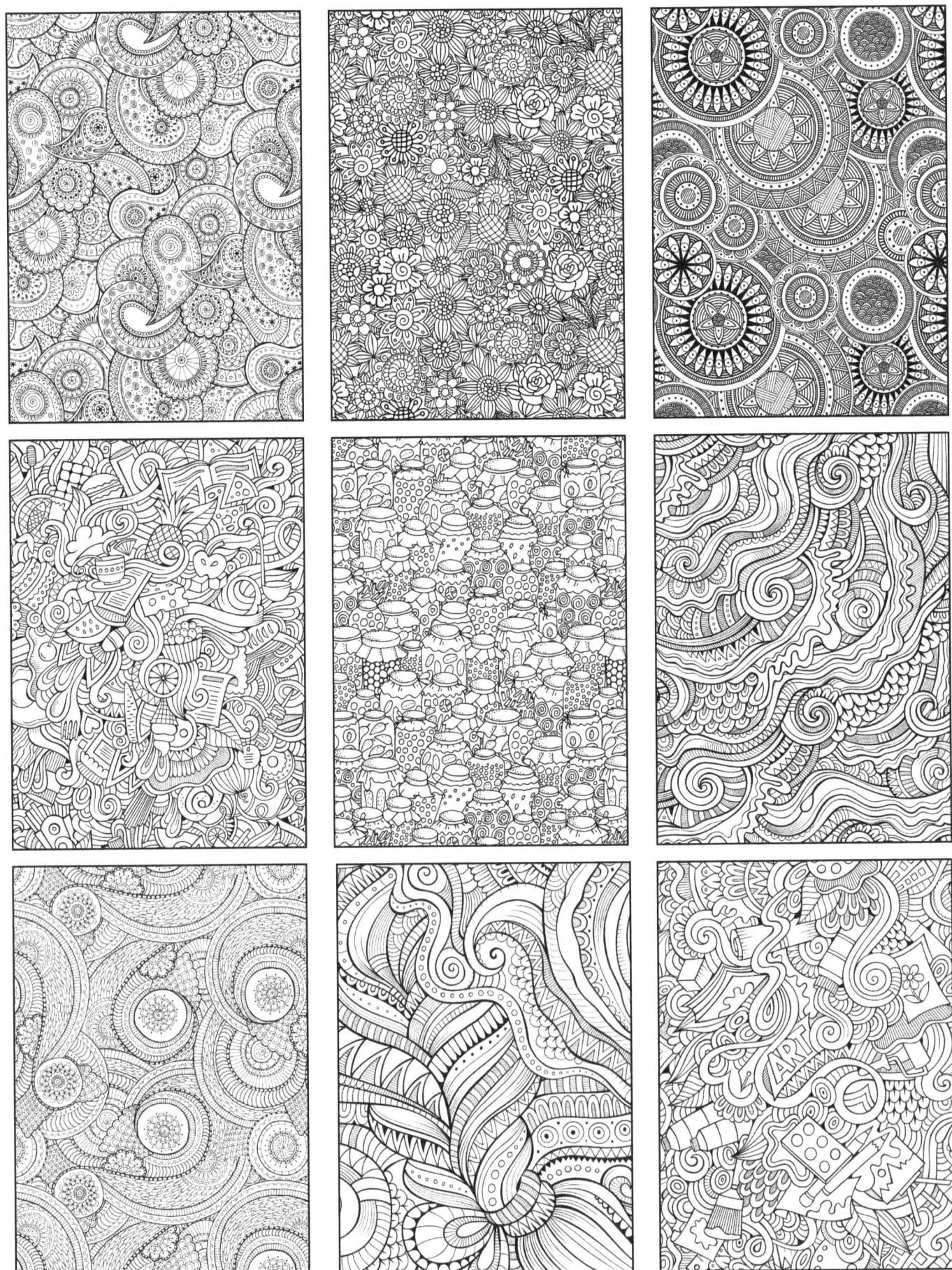

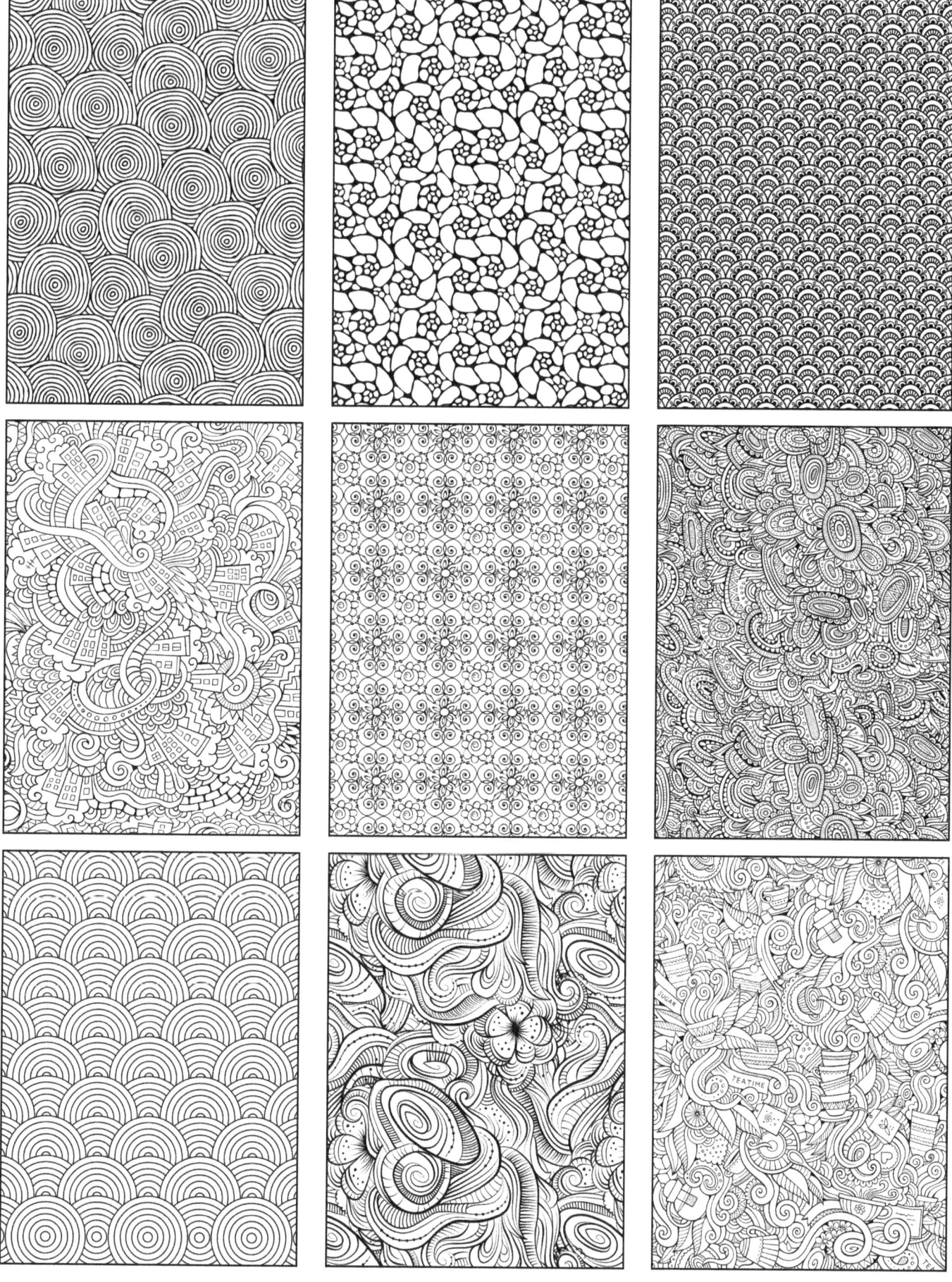

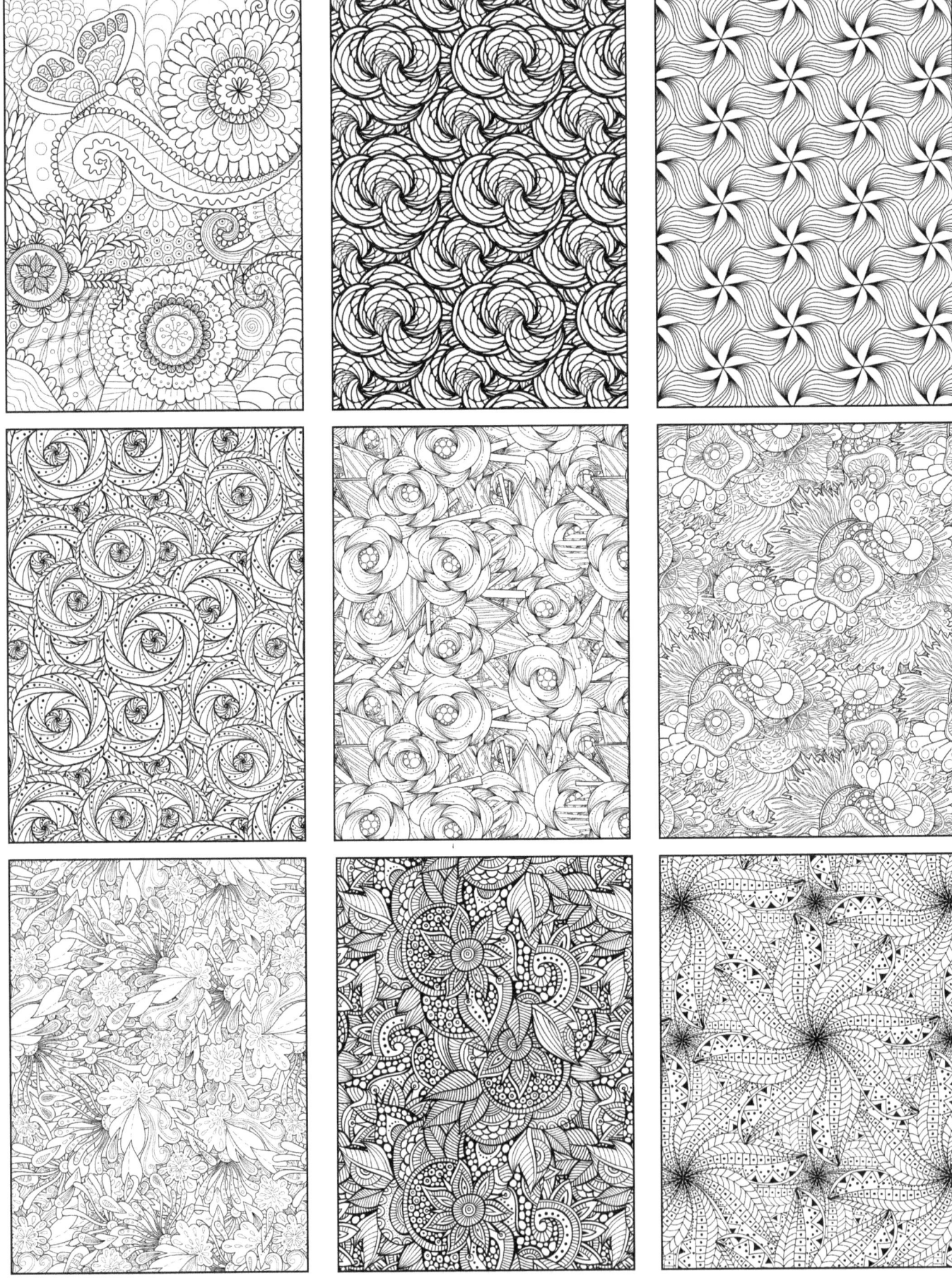

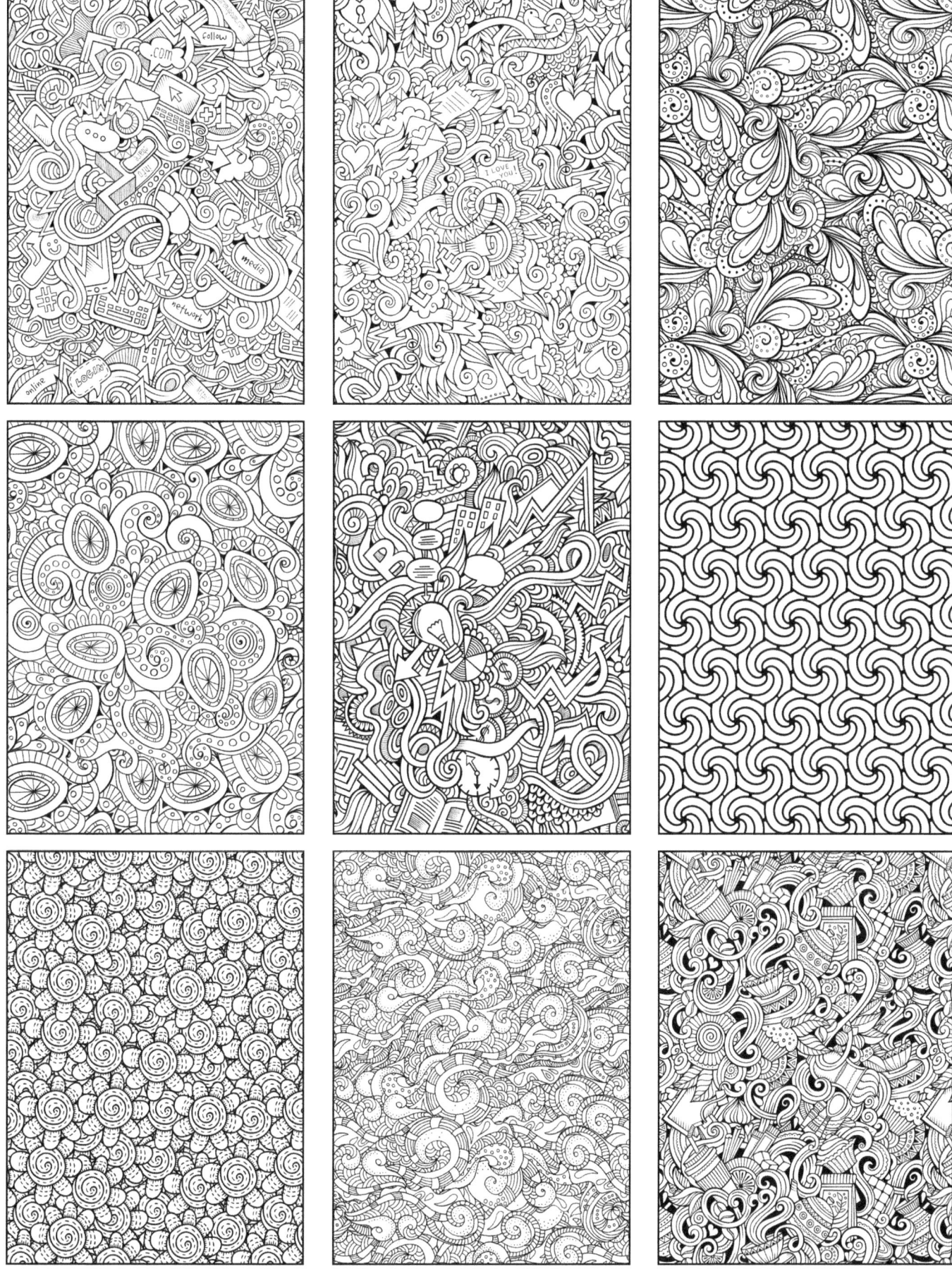

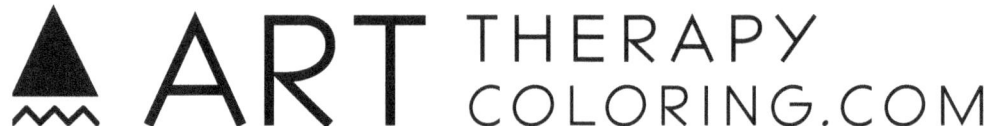

# Did You Enjoy Our Coloring Book?

# We Want To Hear About It!

Help spread the word about our adult coloring books! We give 10% of all proceeds from Art Therapy products to benefit pancreatic cancer patients and their families.

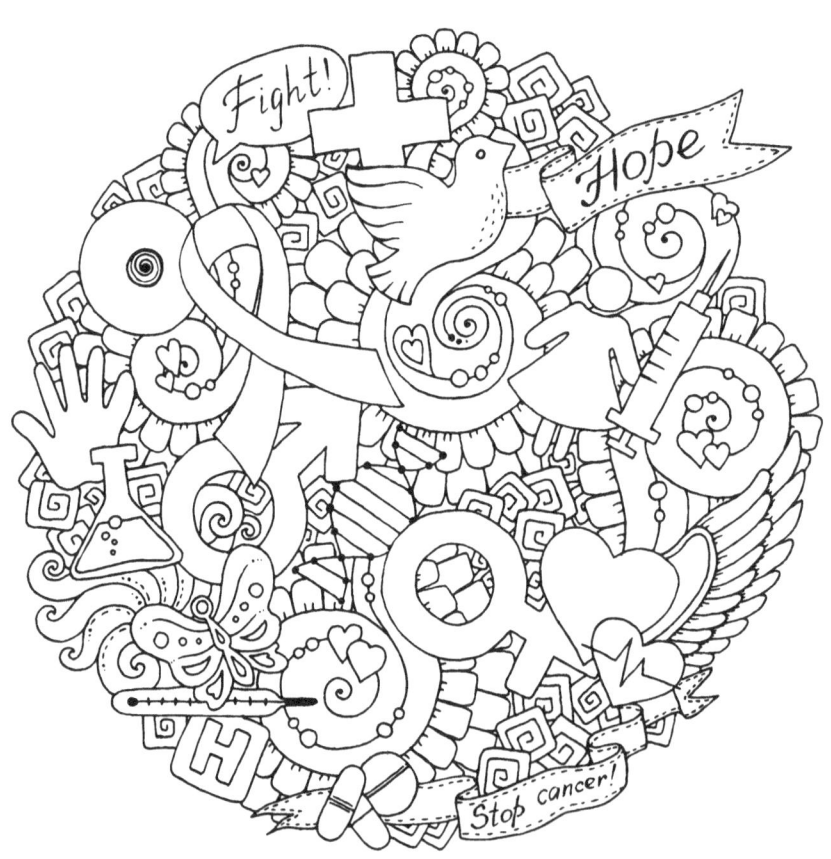

The best way to spread the word is through reviews. We know how busy you are, especially with all of that coloring, but we would appreciate it!

Visit our website at **www.arttherapycoloring.com**

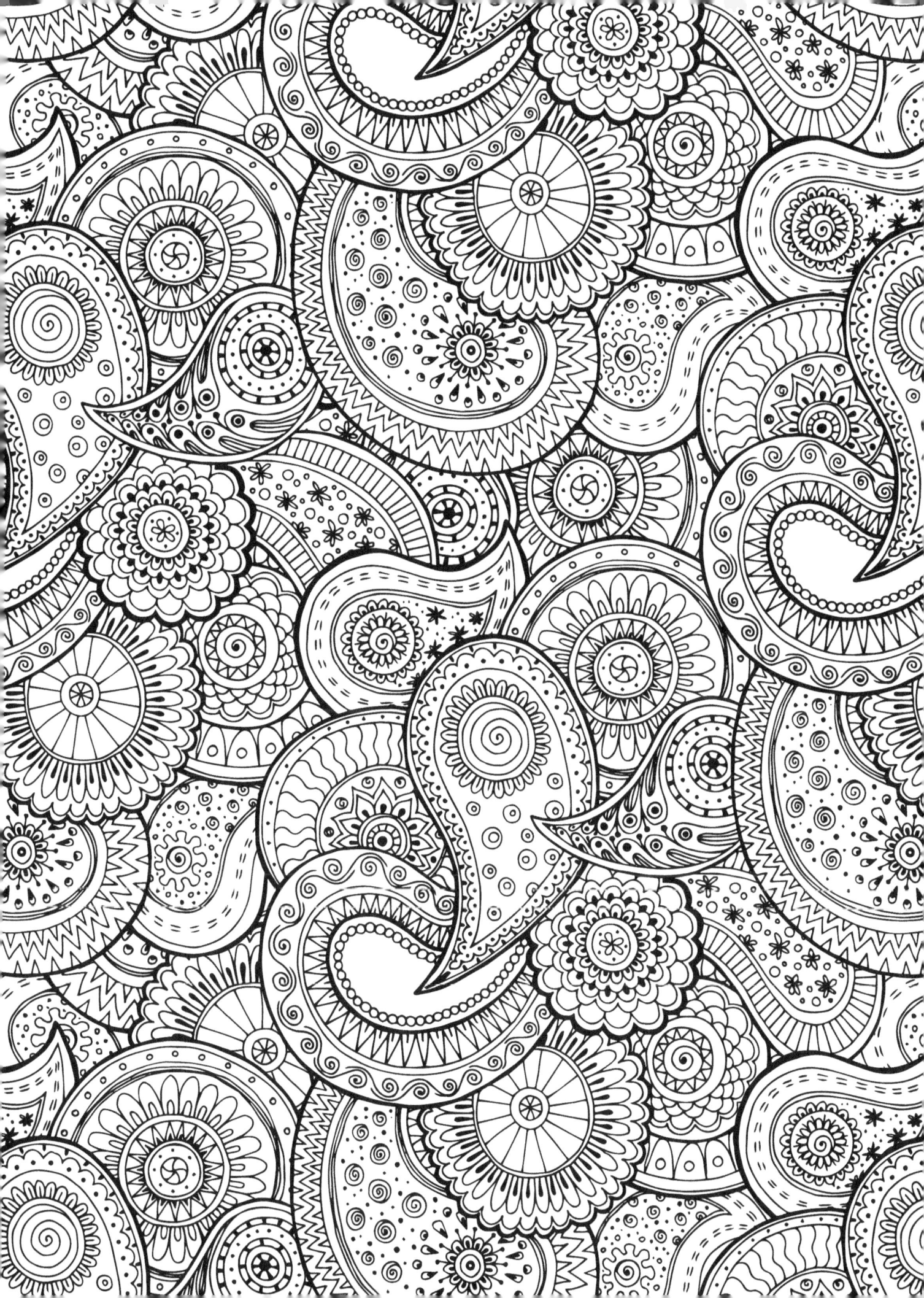

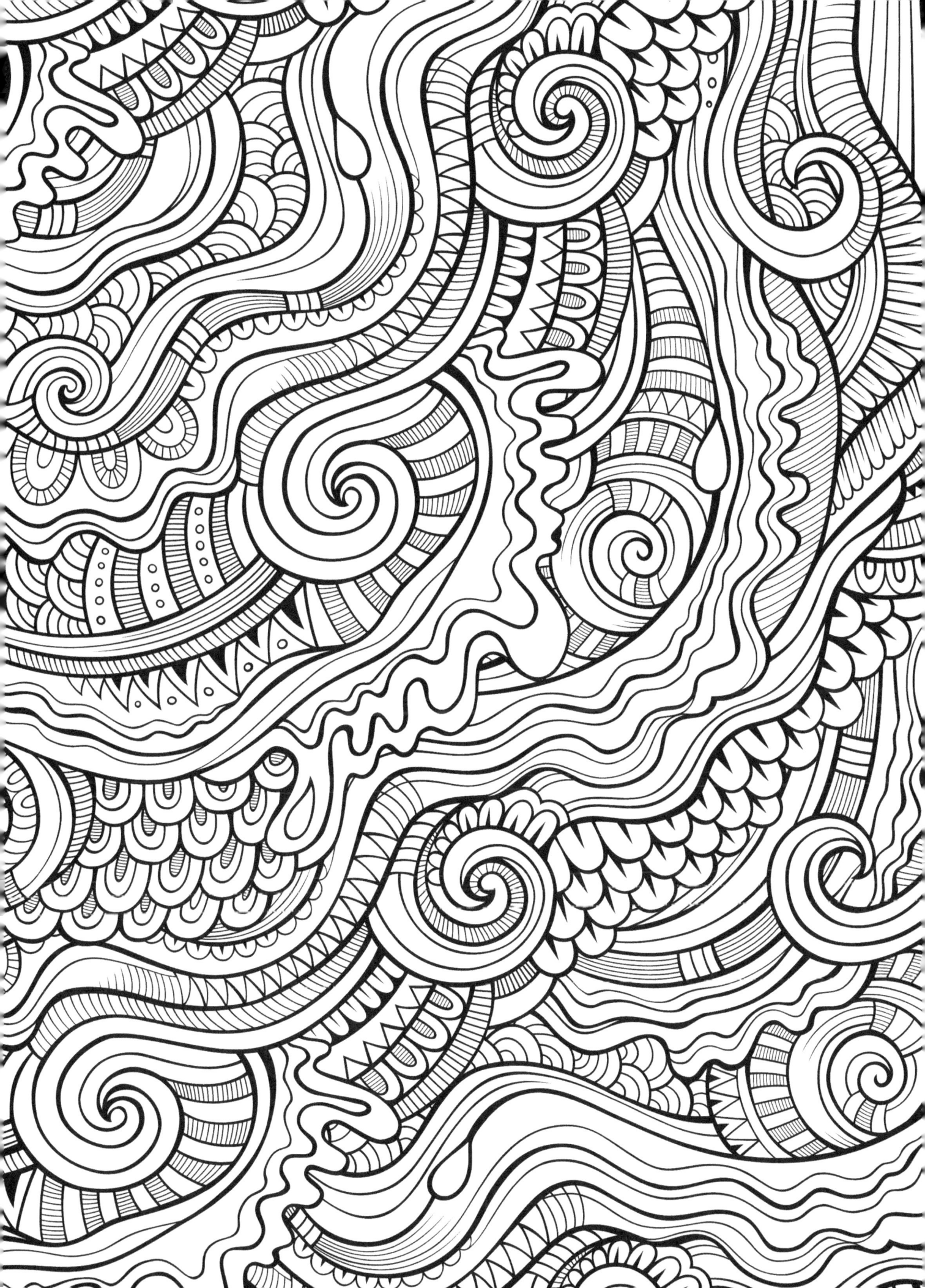

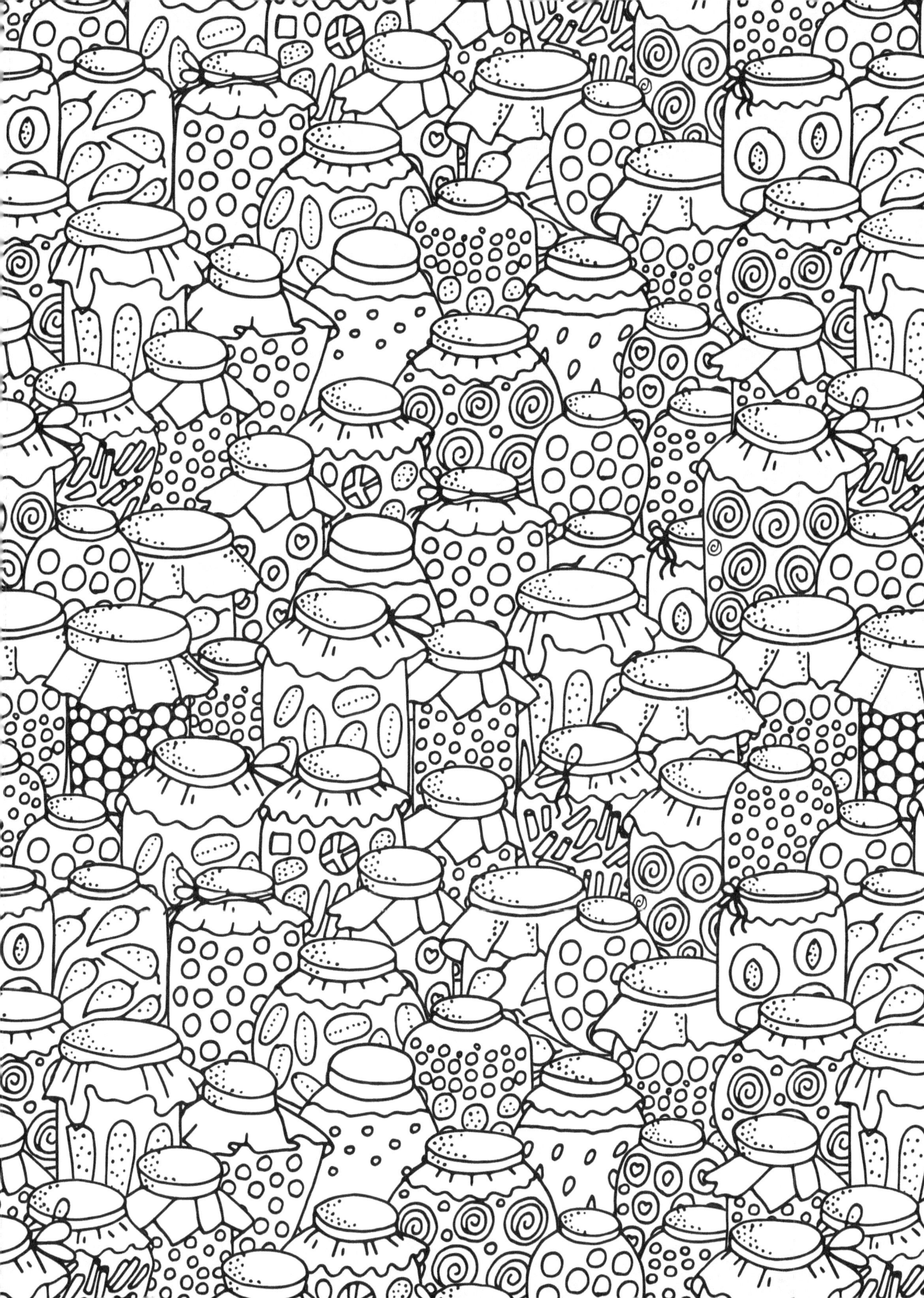

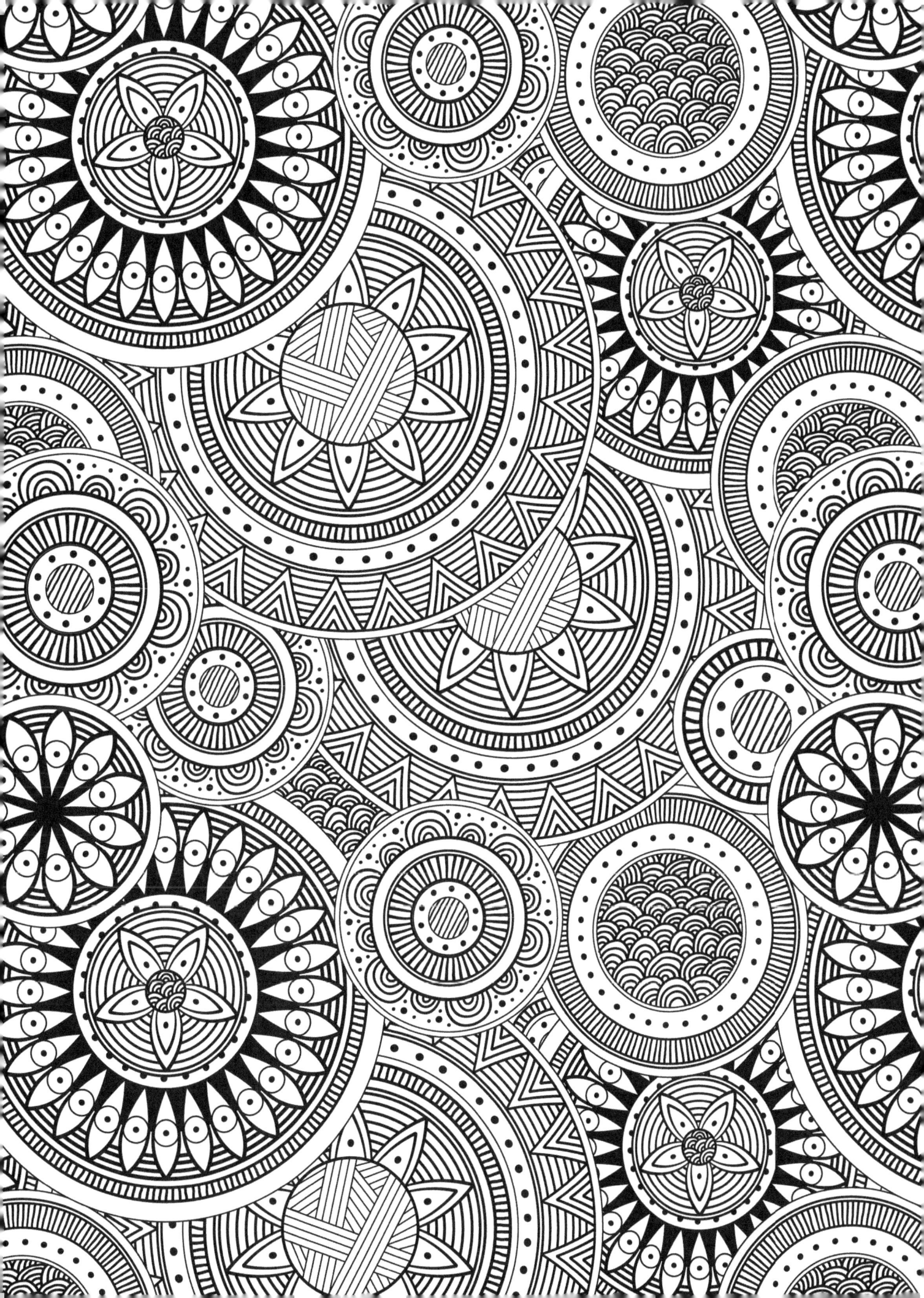

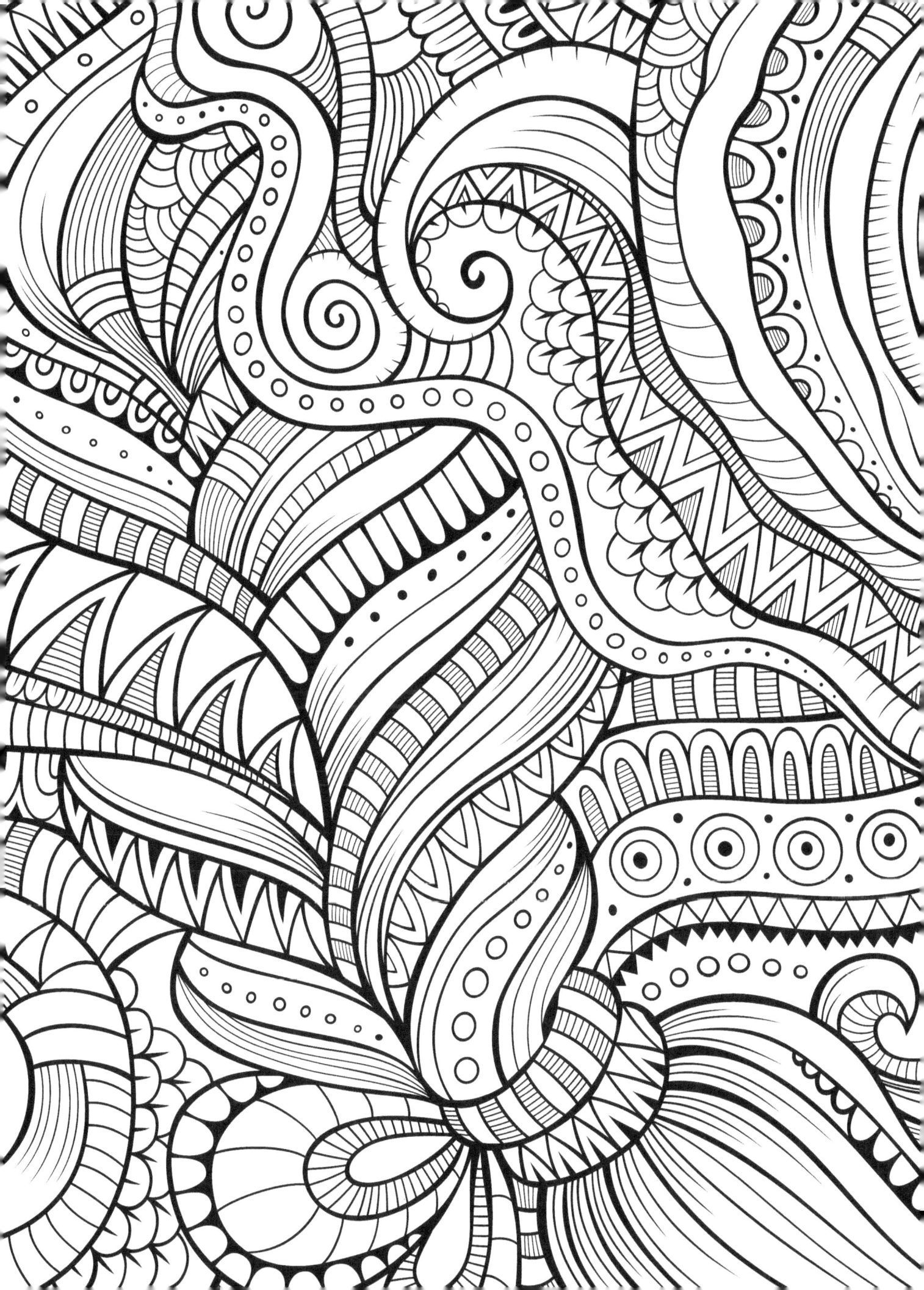

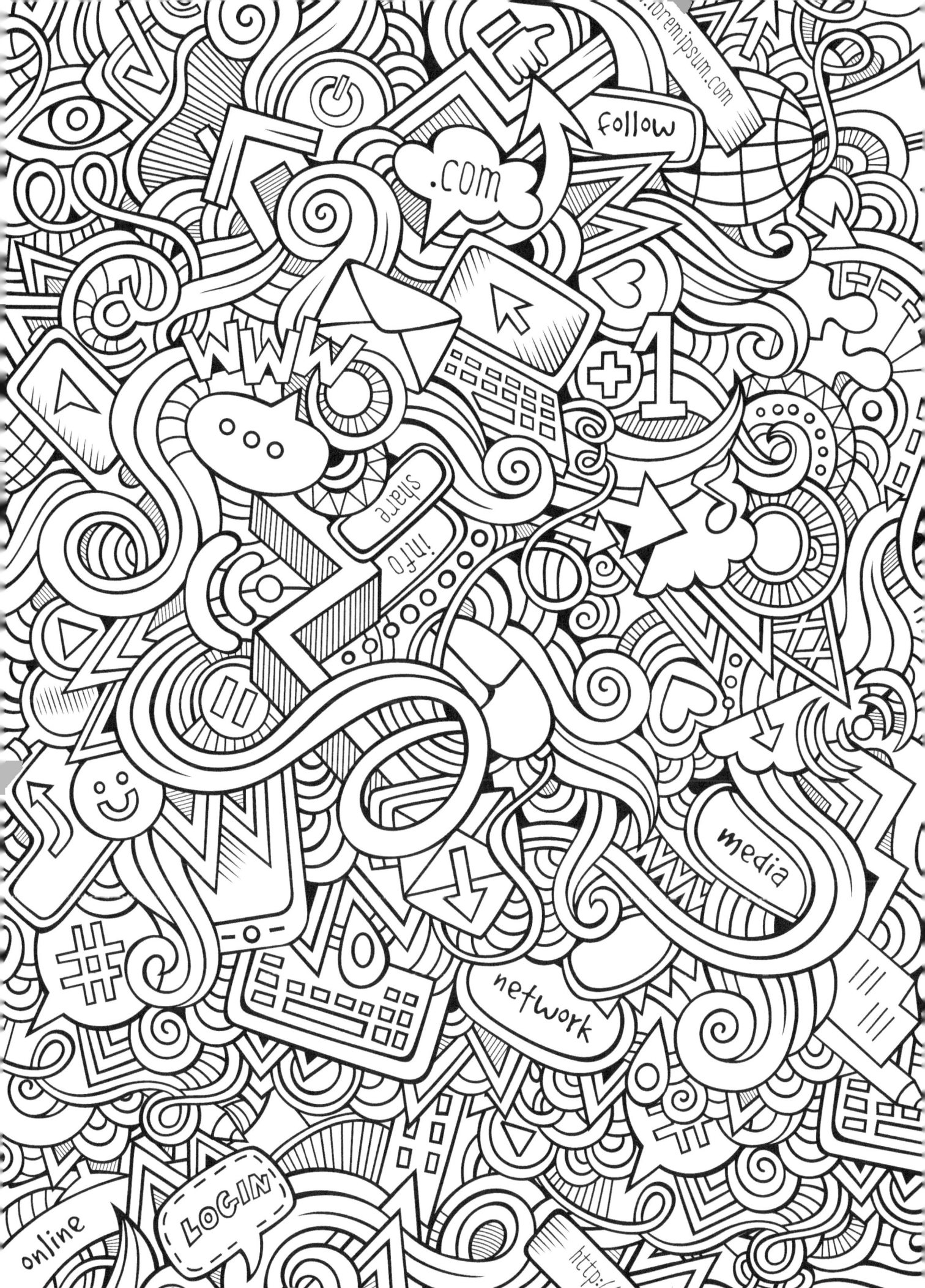

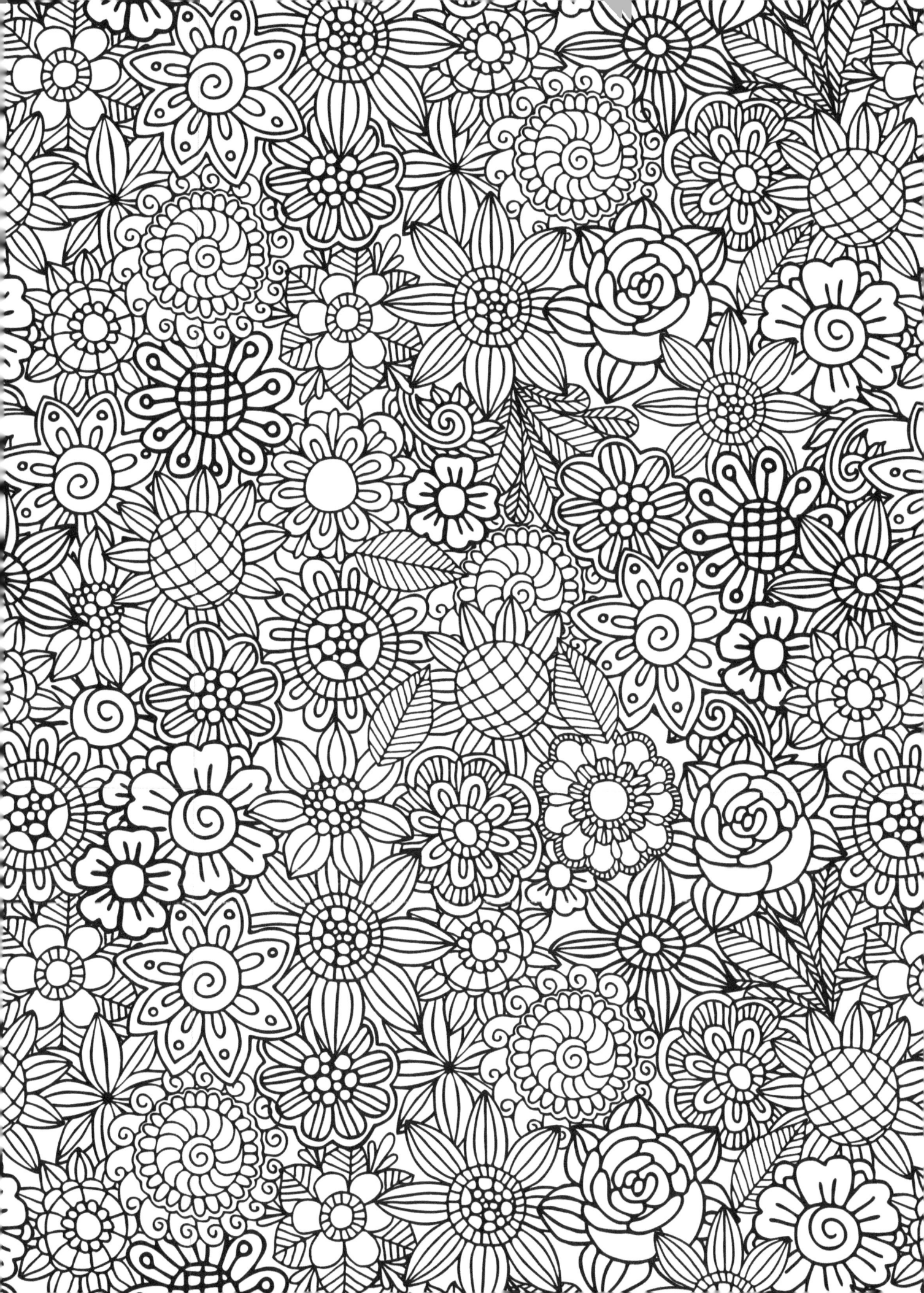

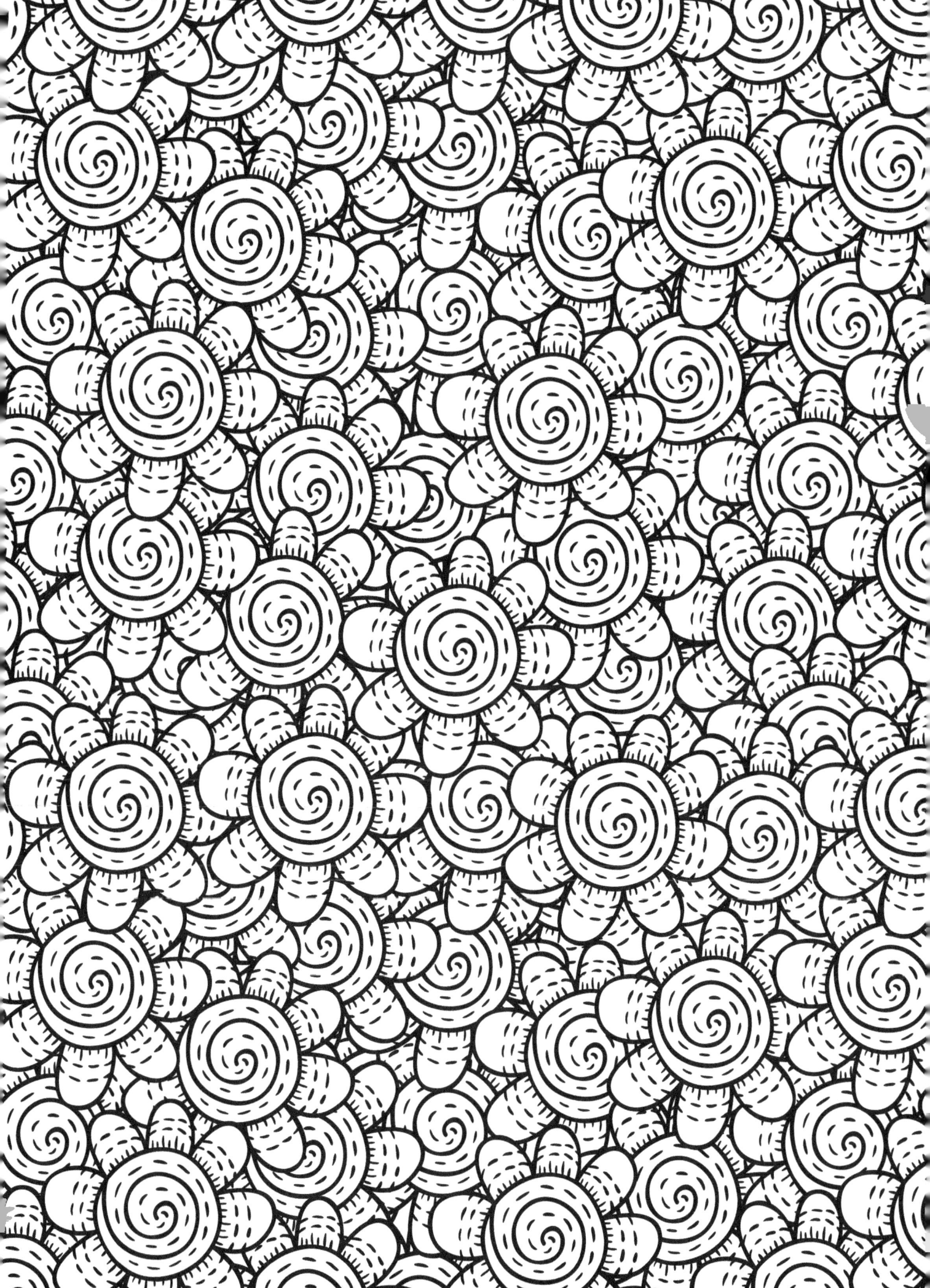

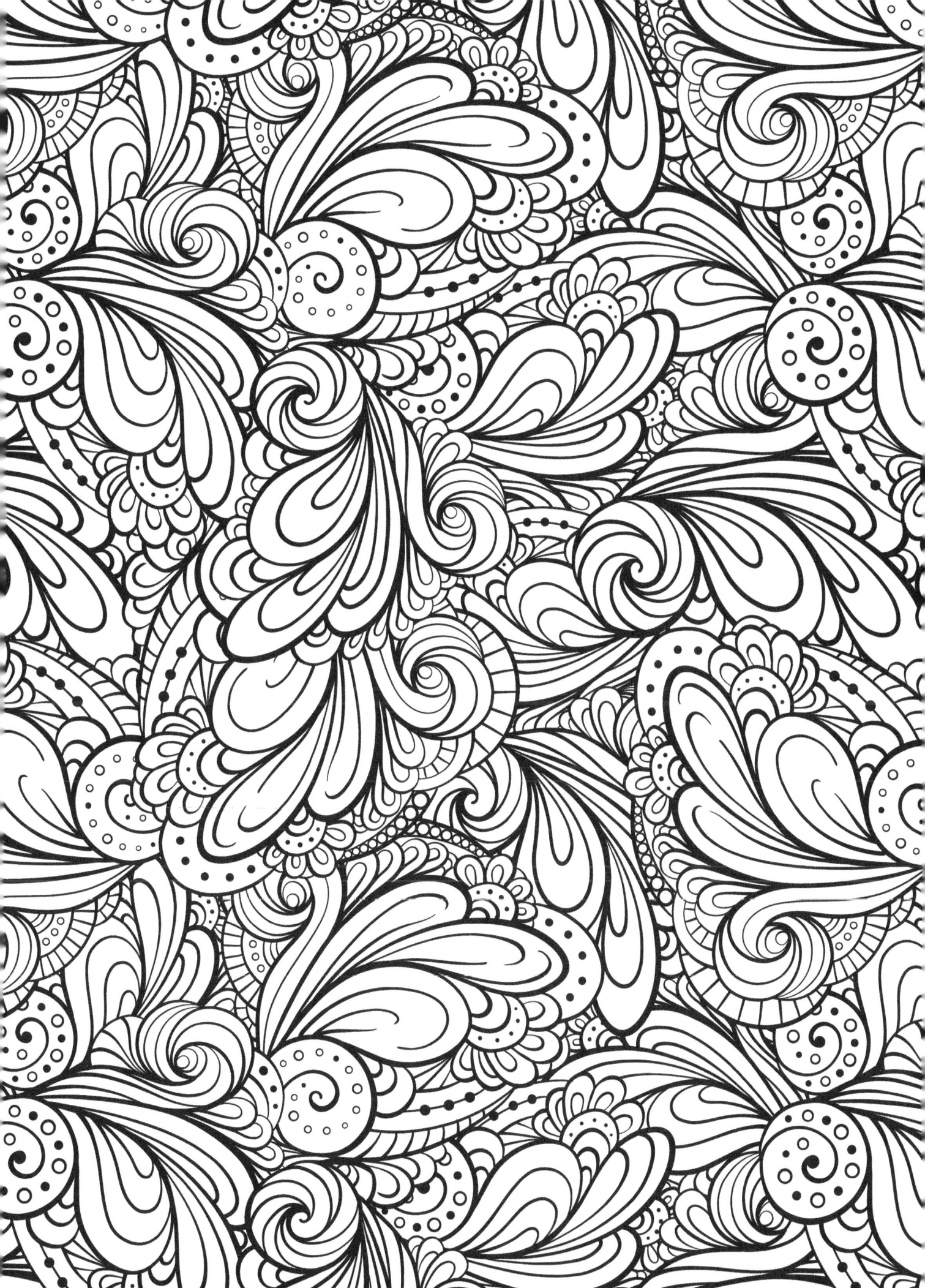

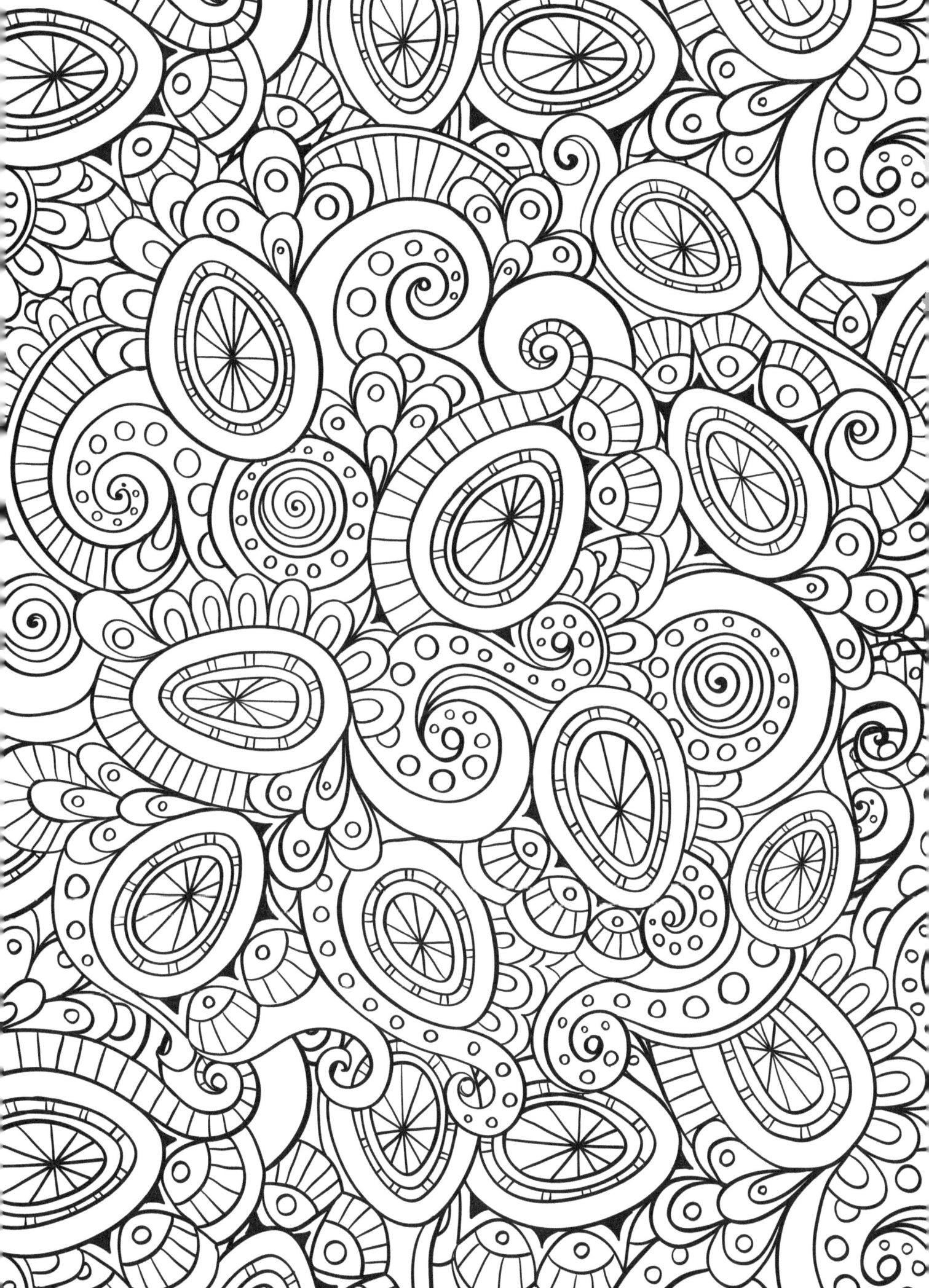

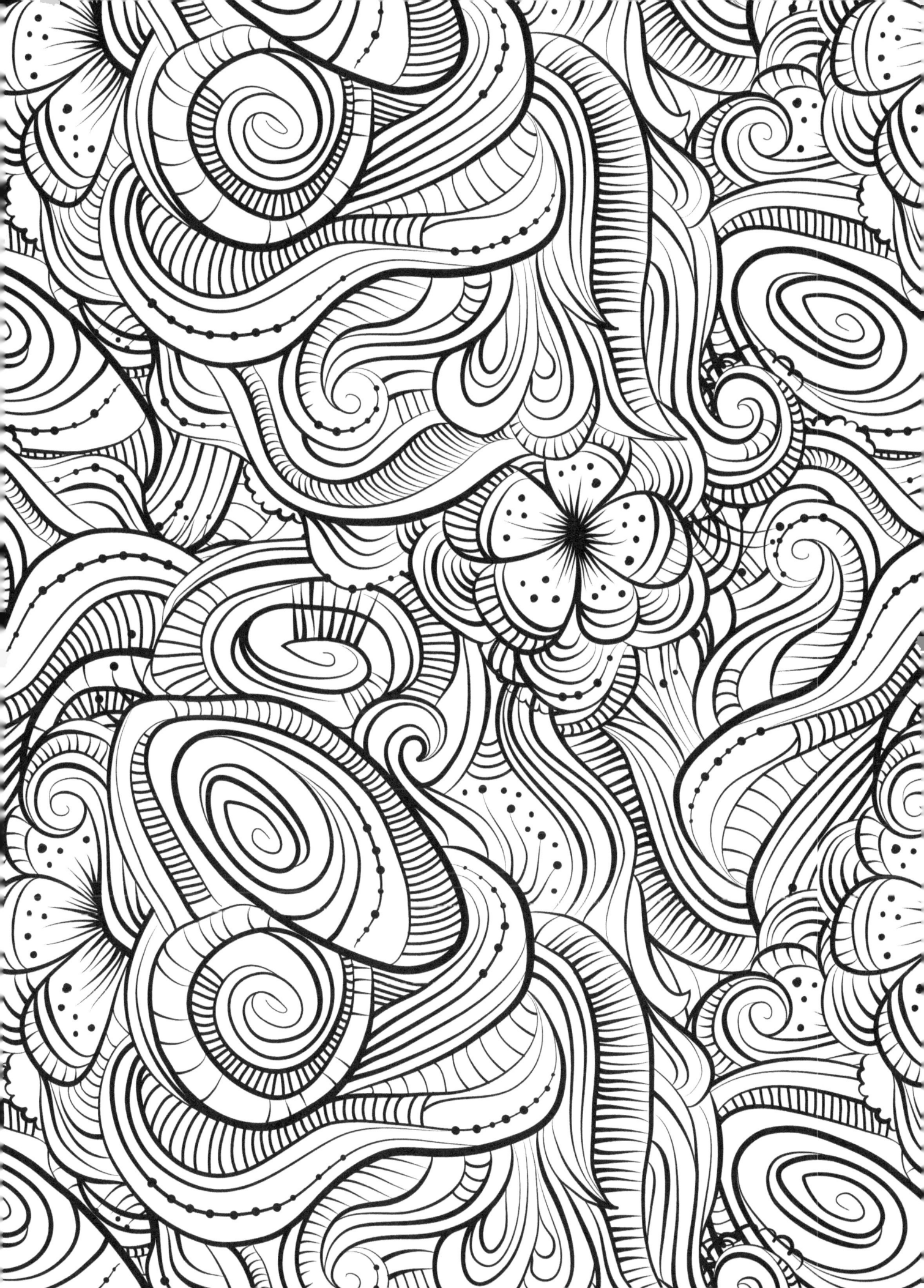

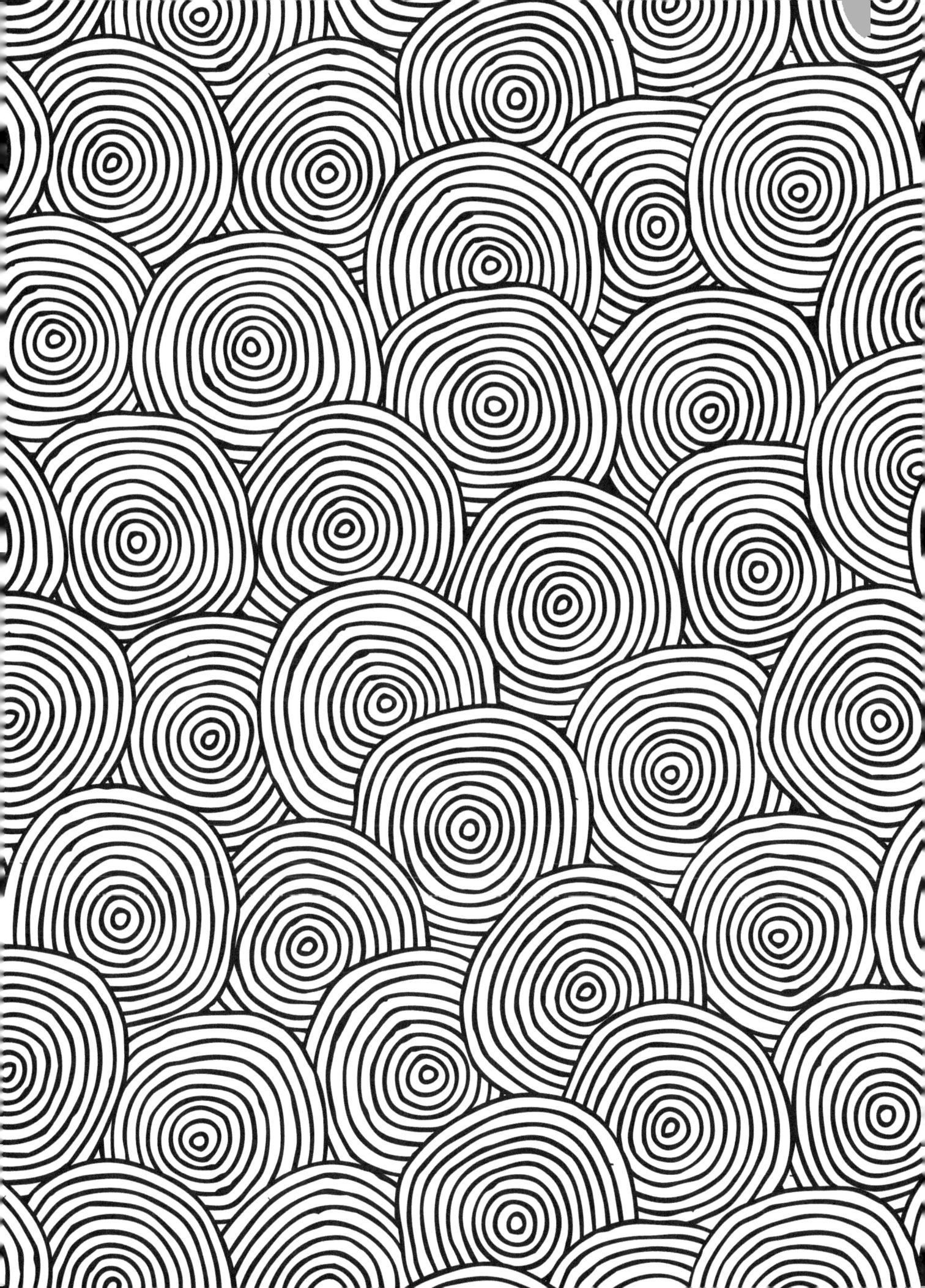

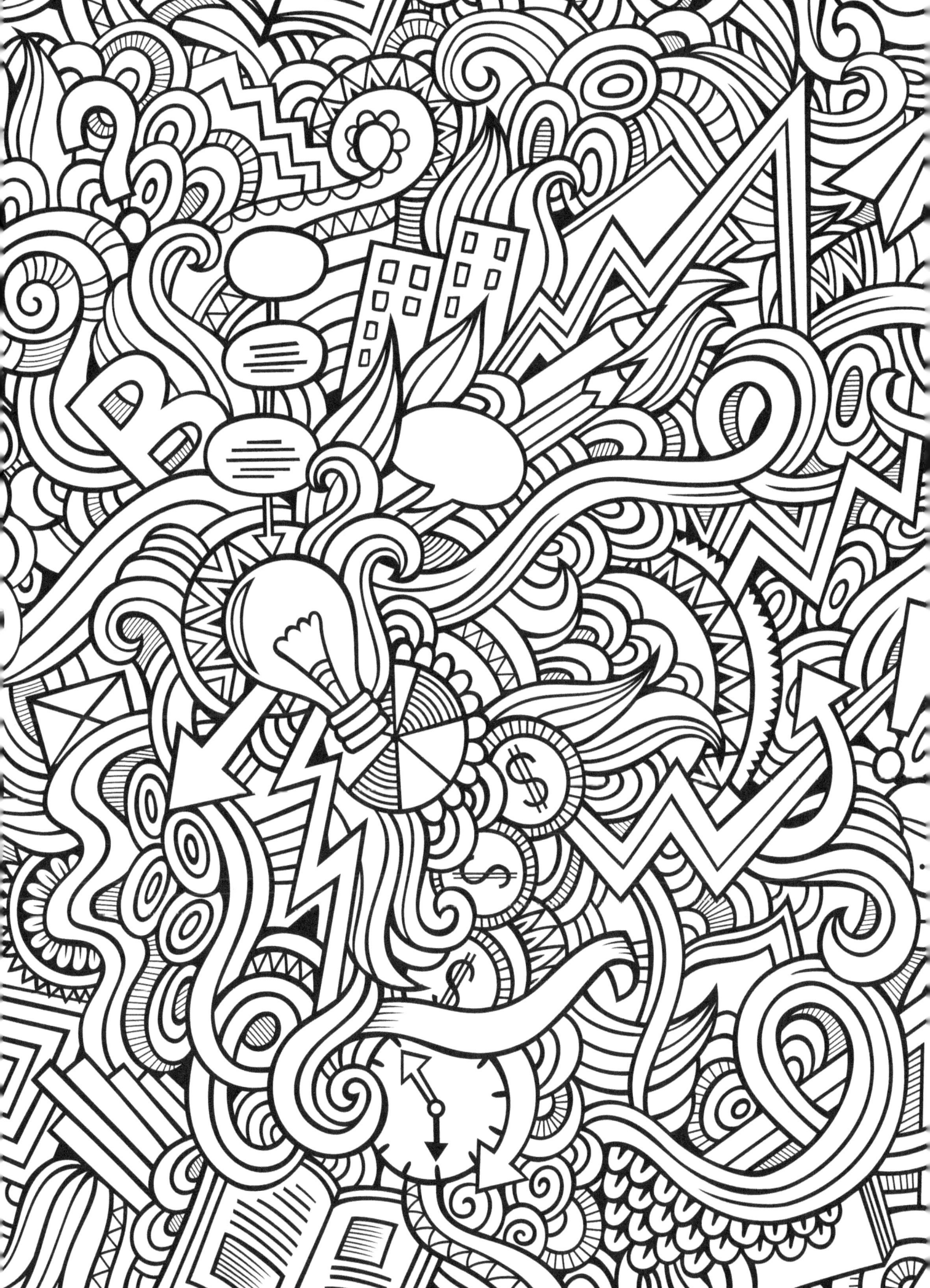

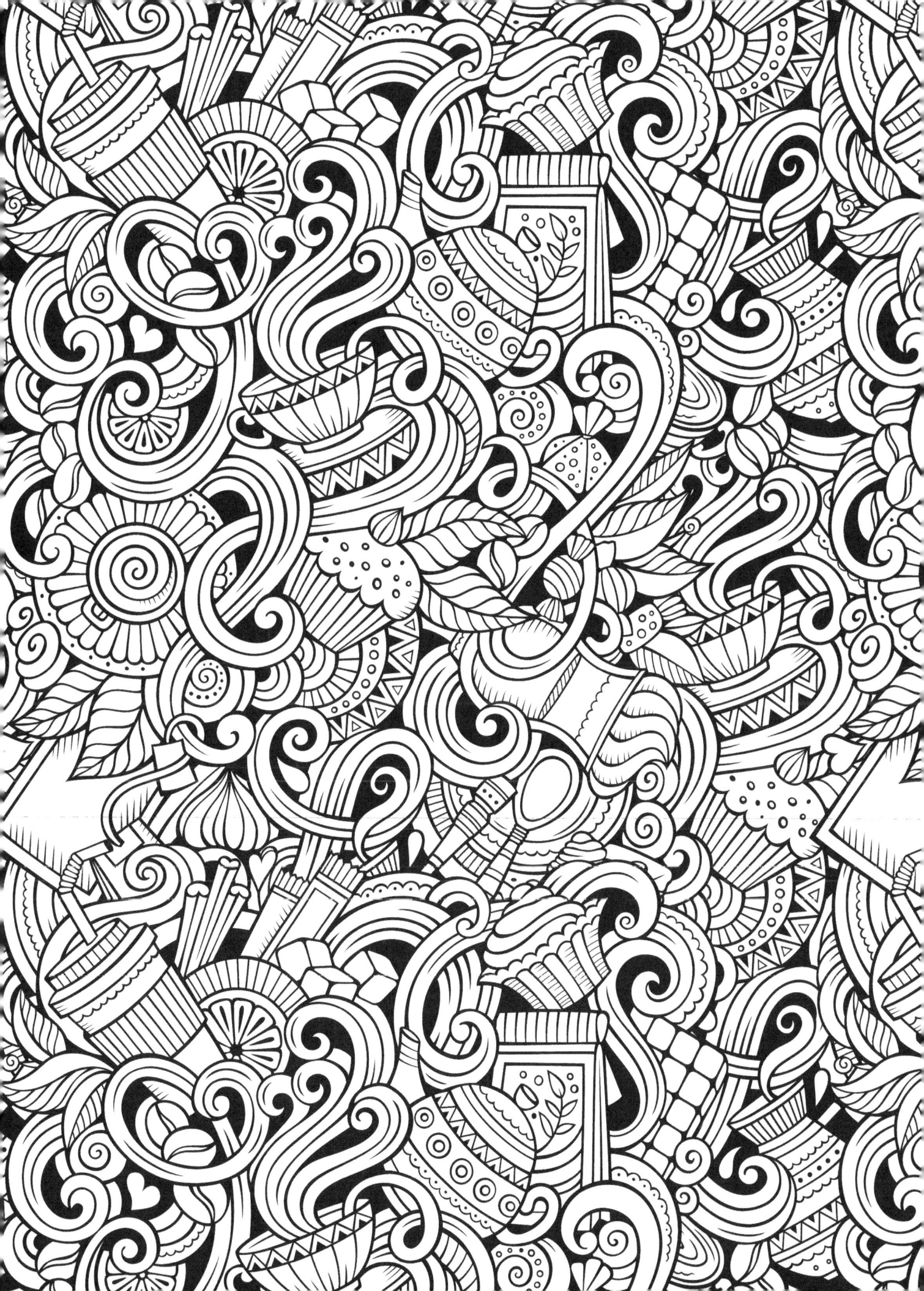

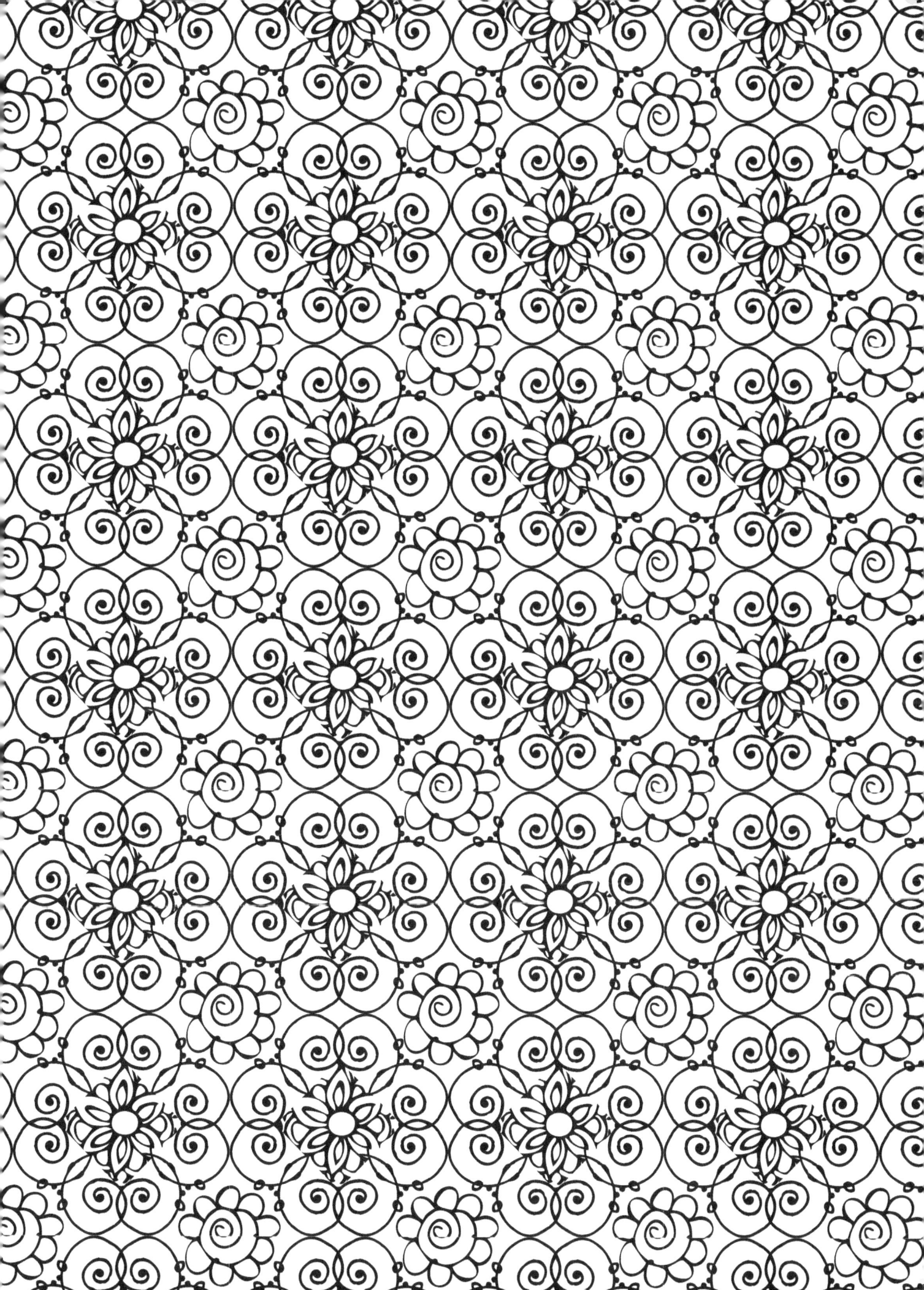

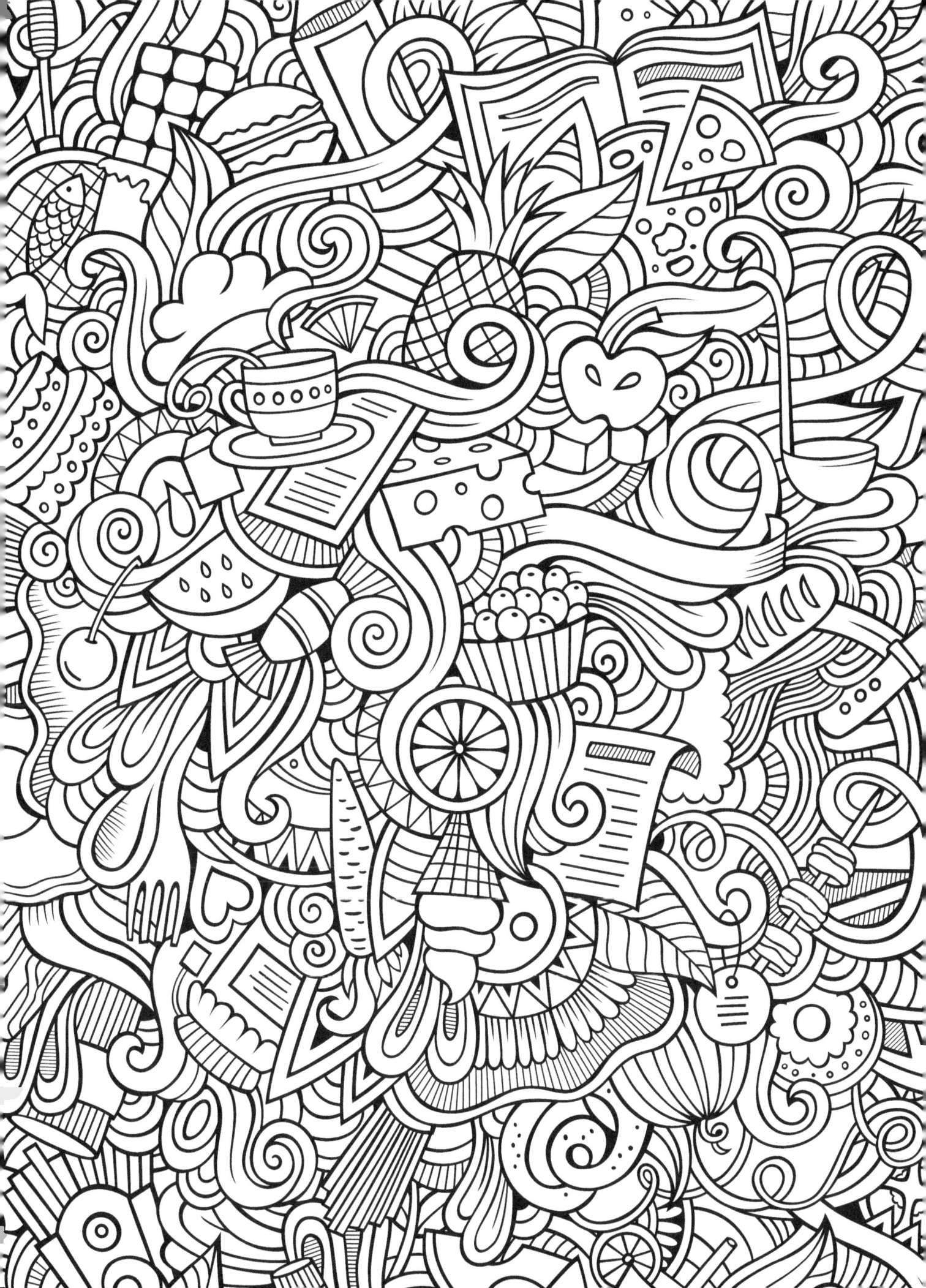

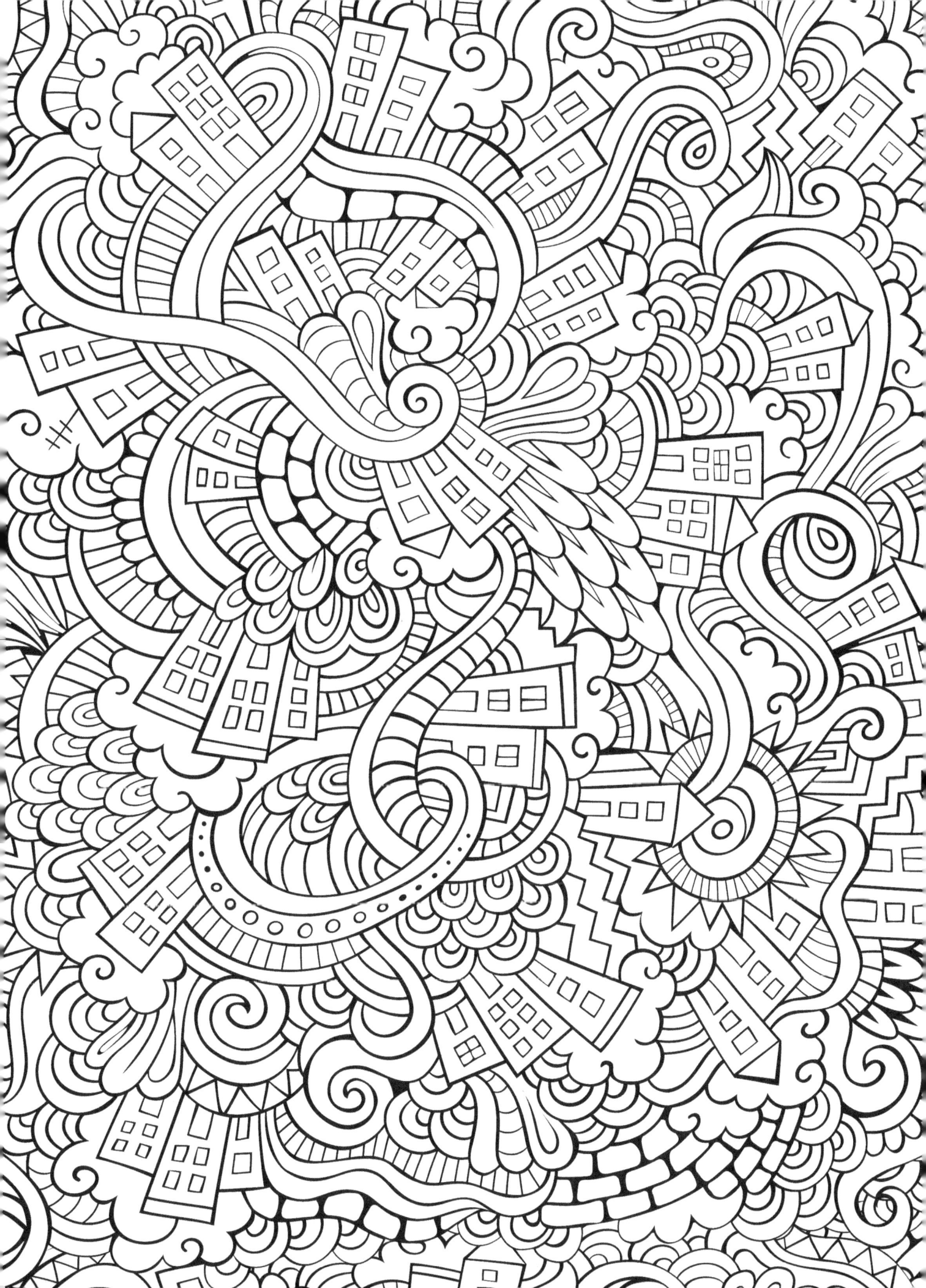

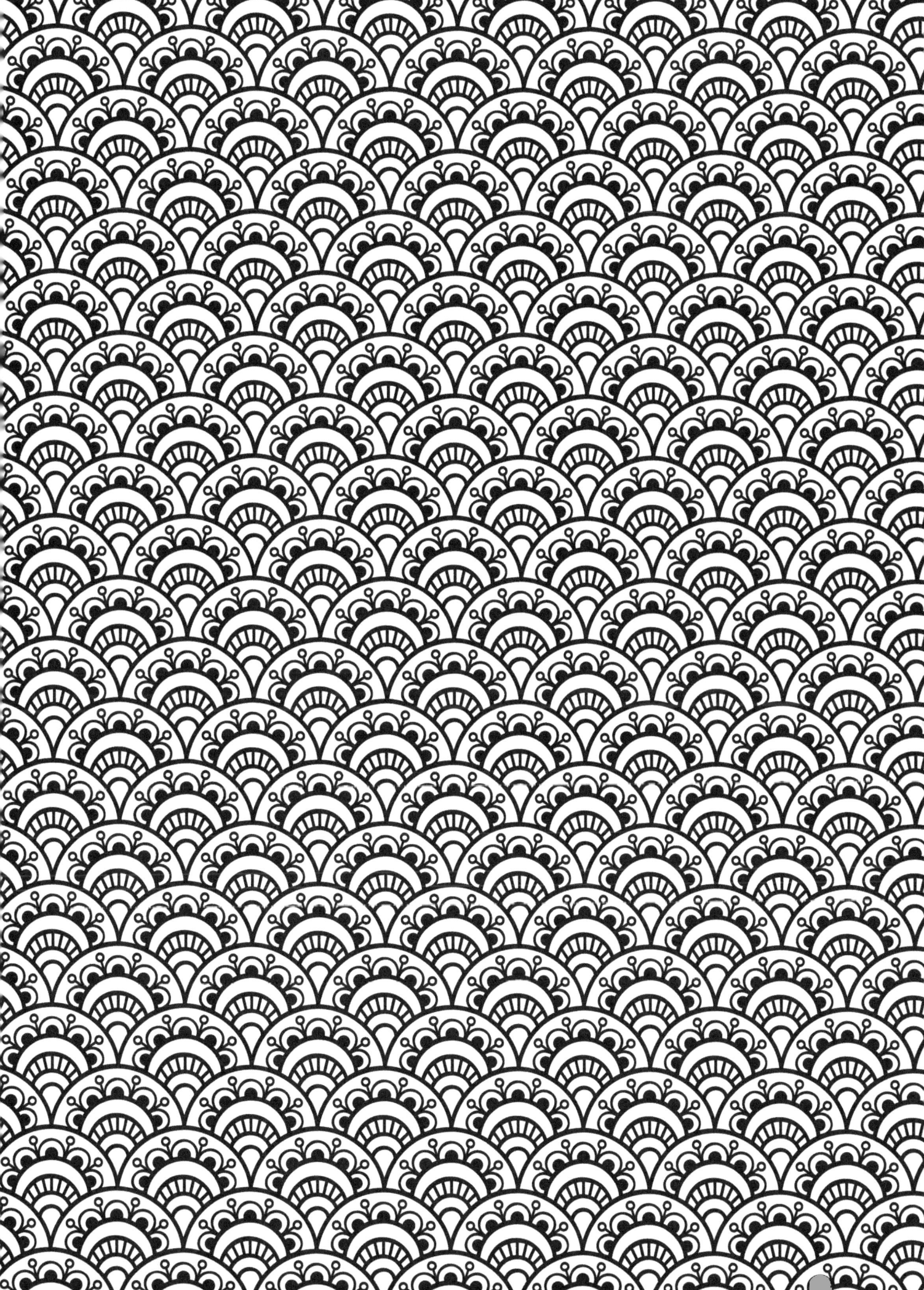

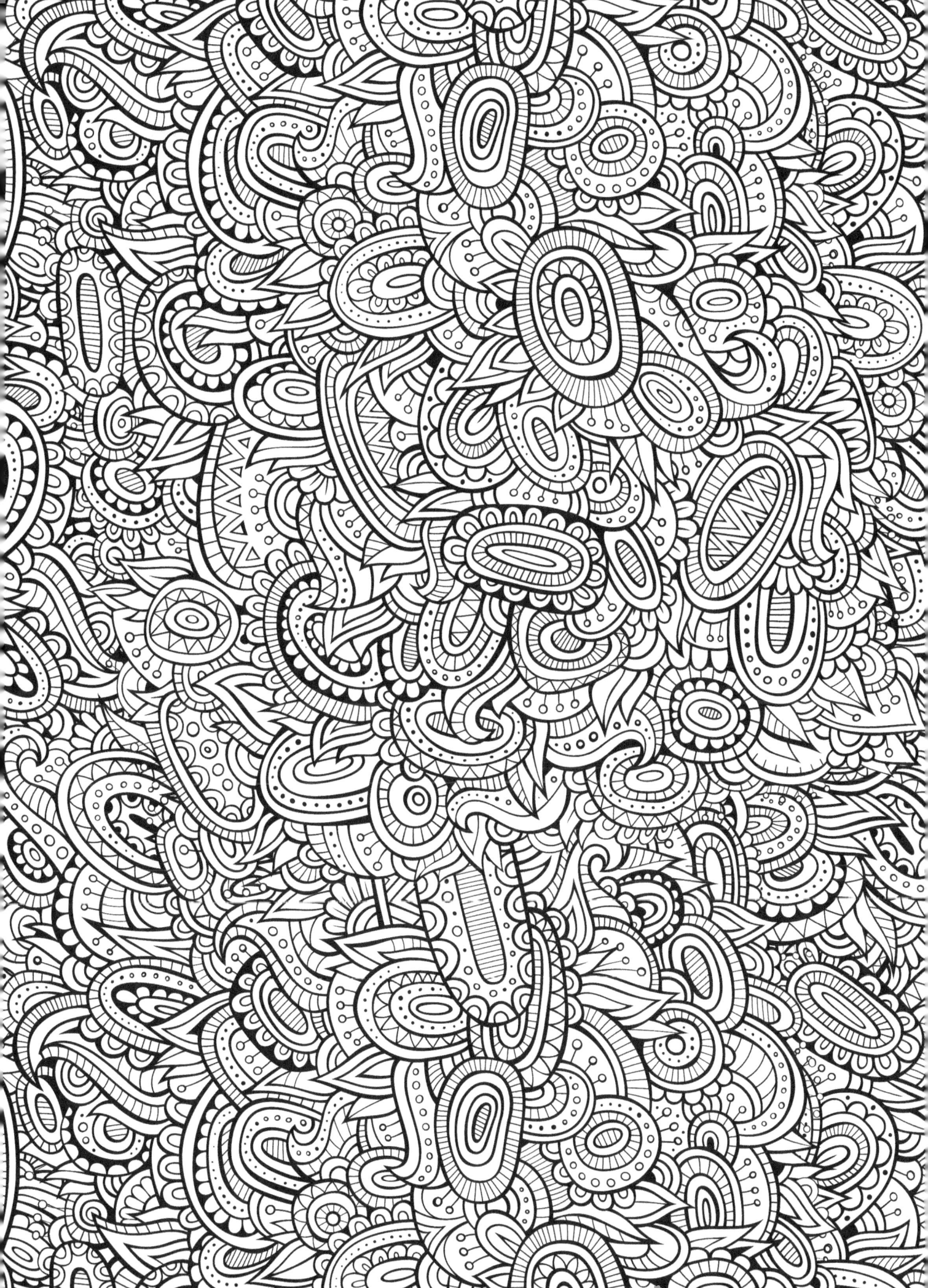

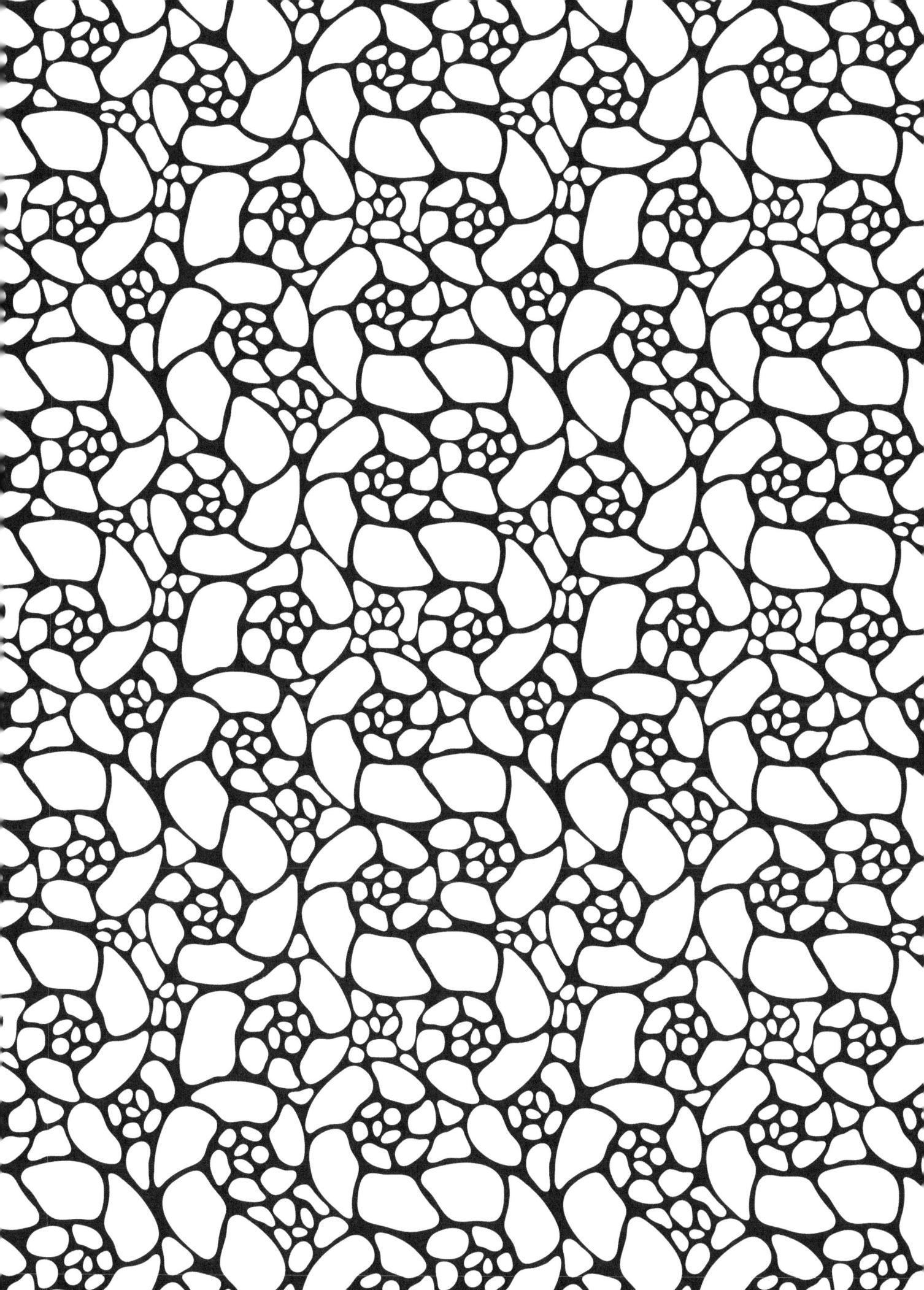

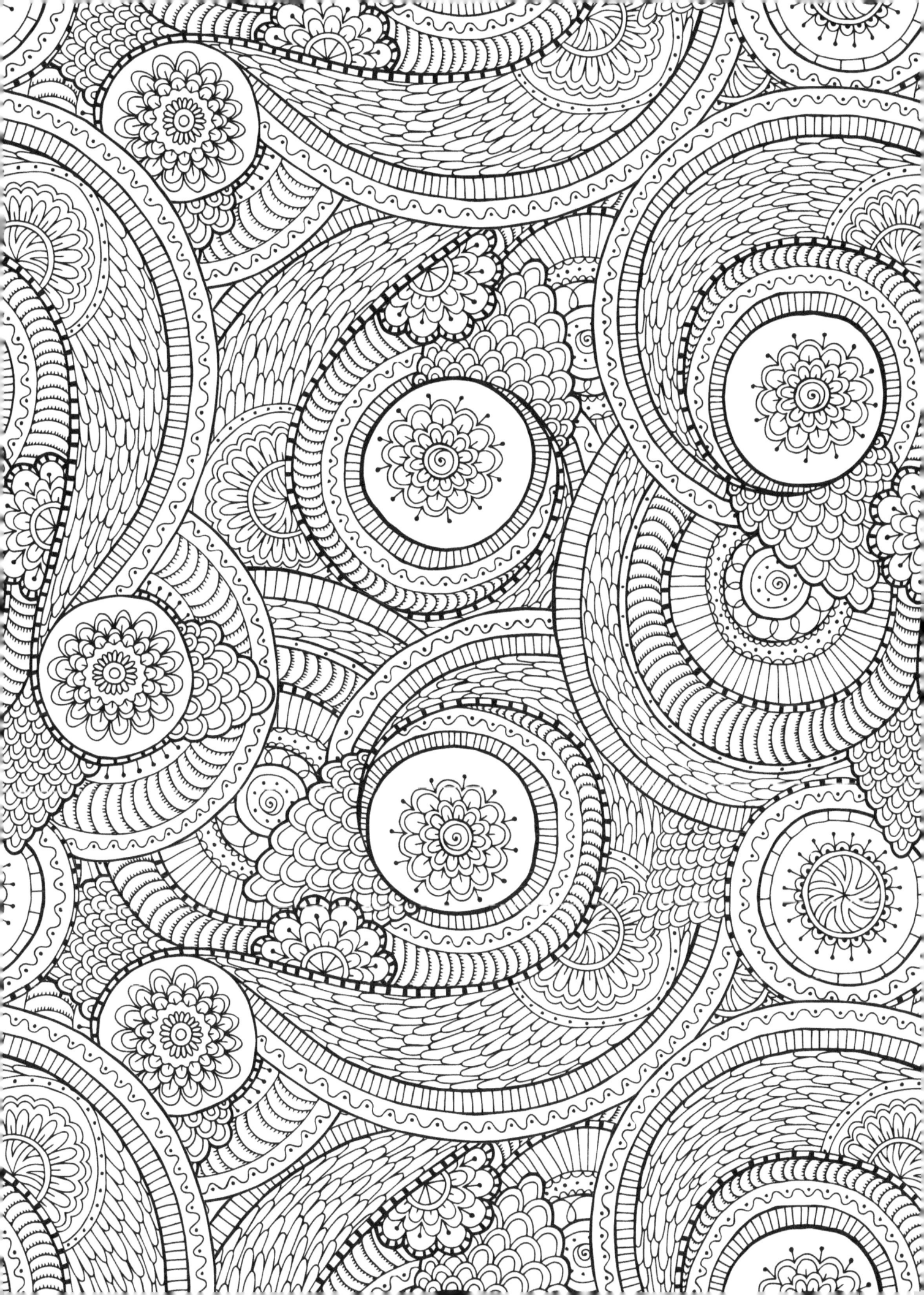

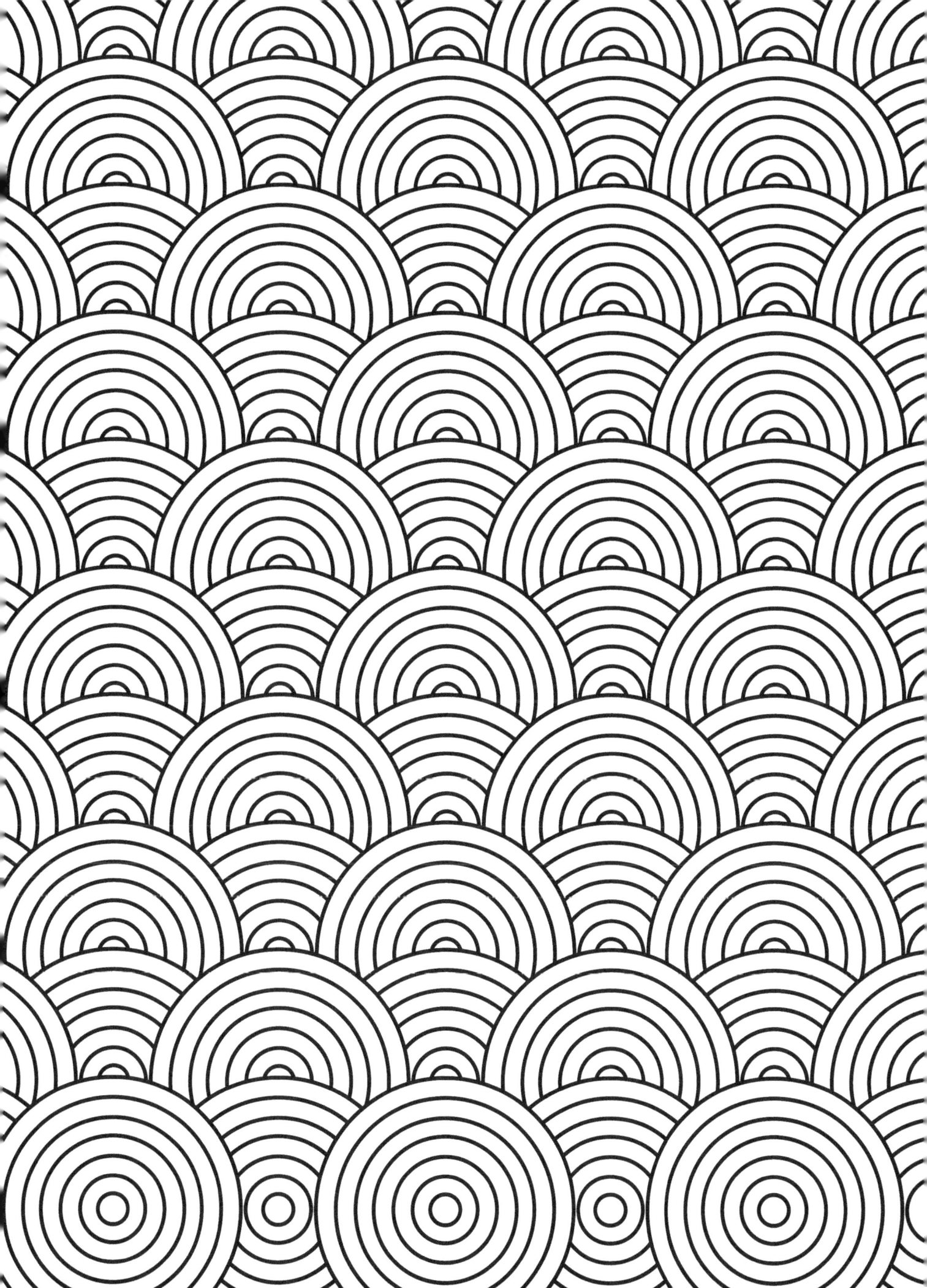

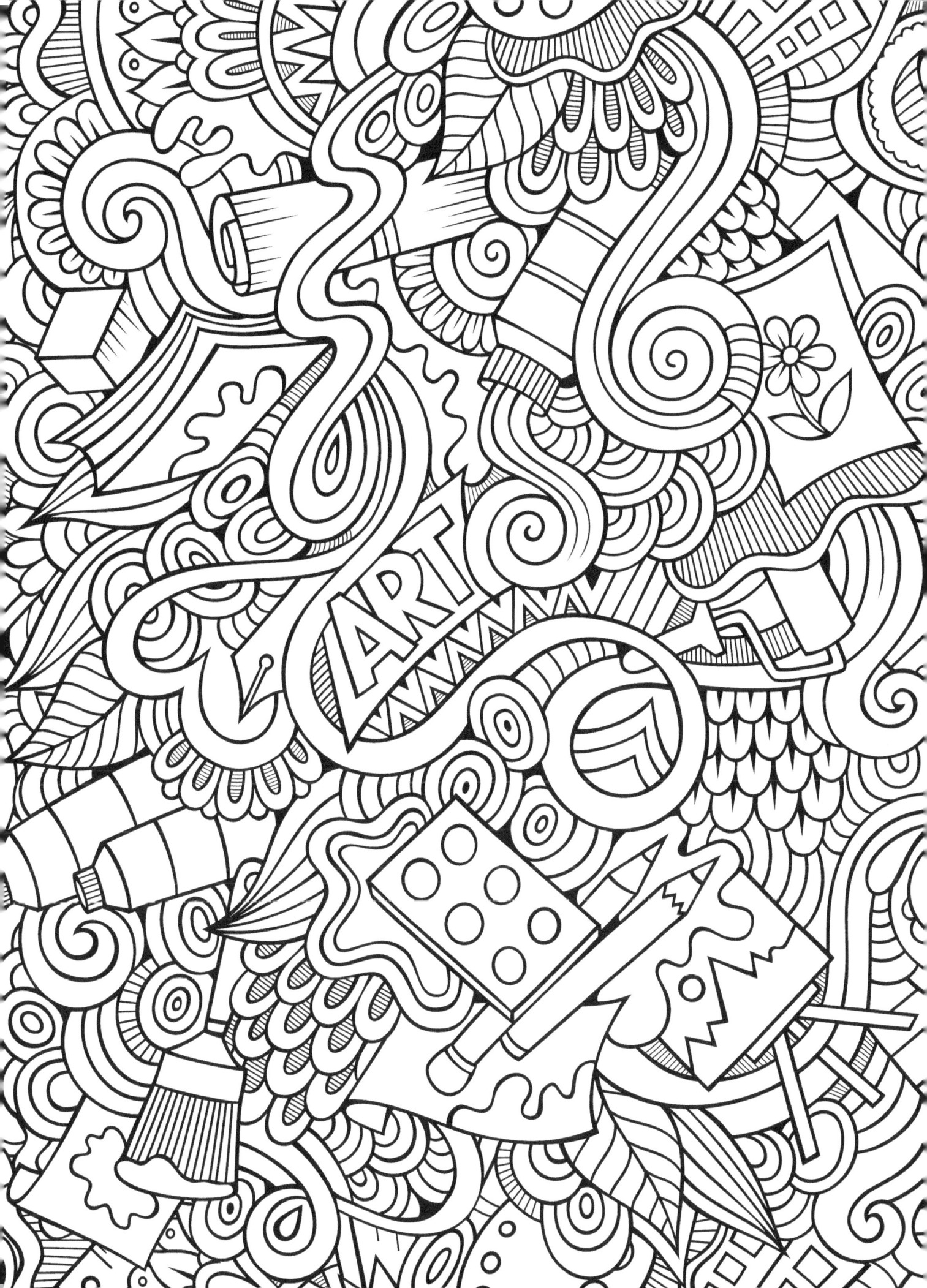

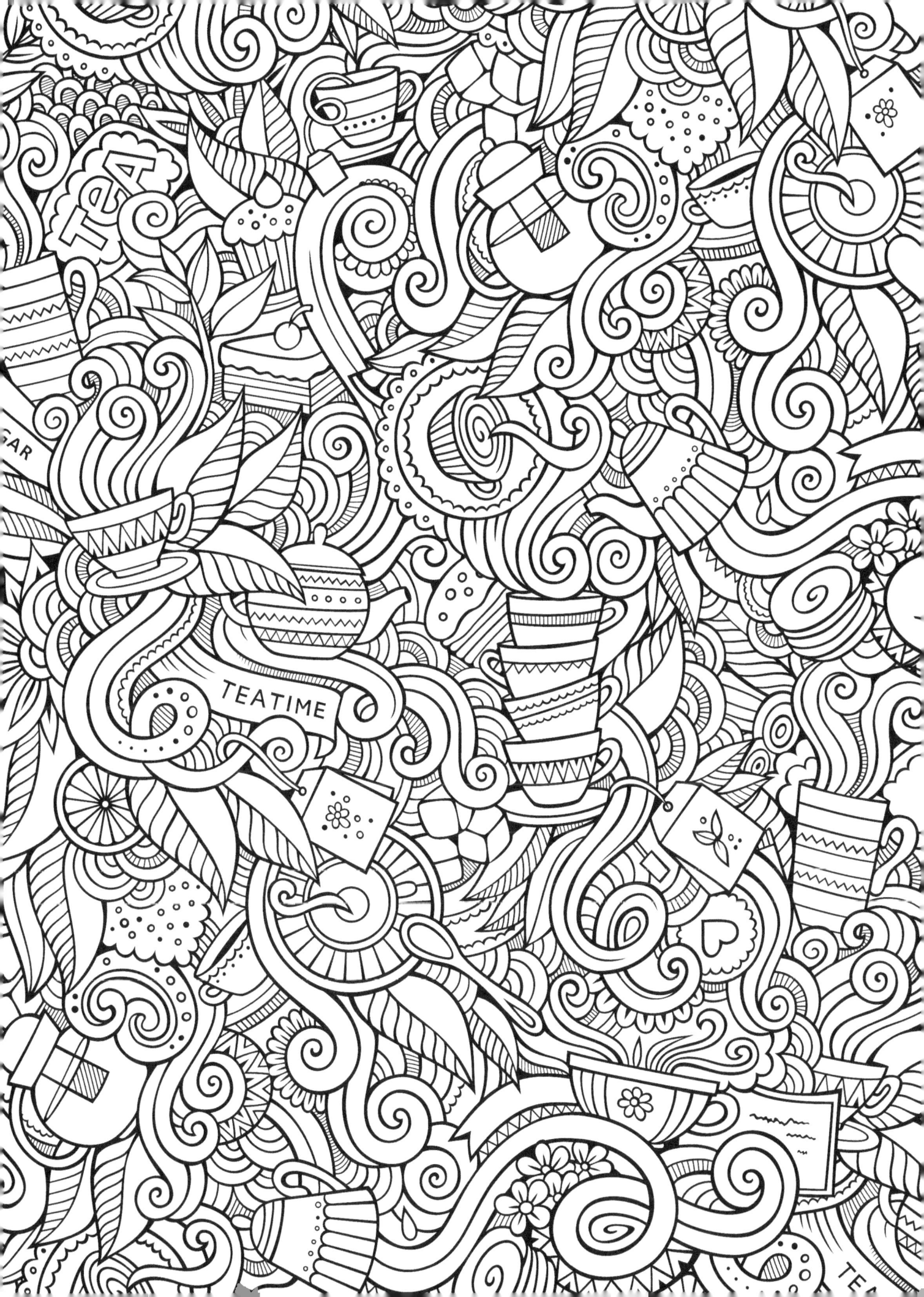

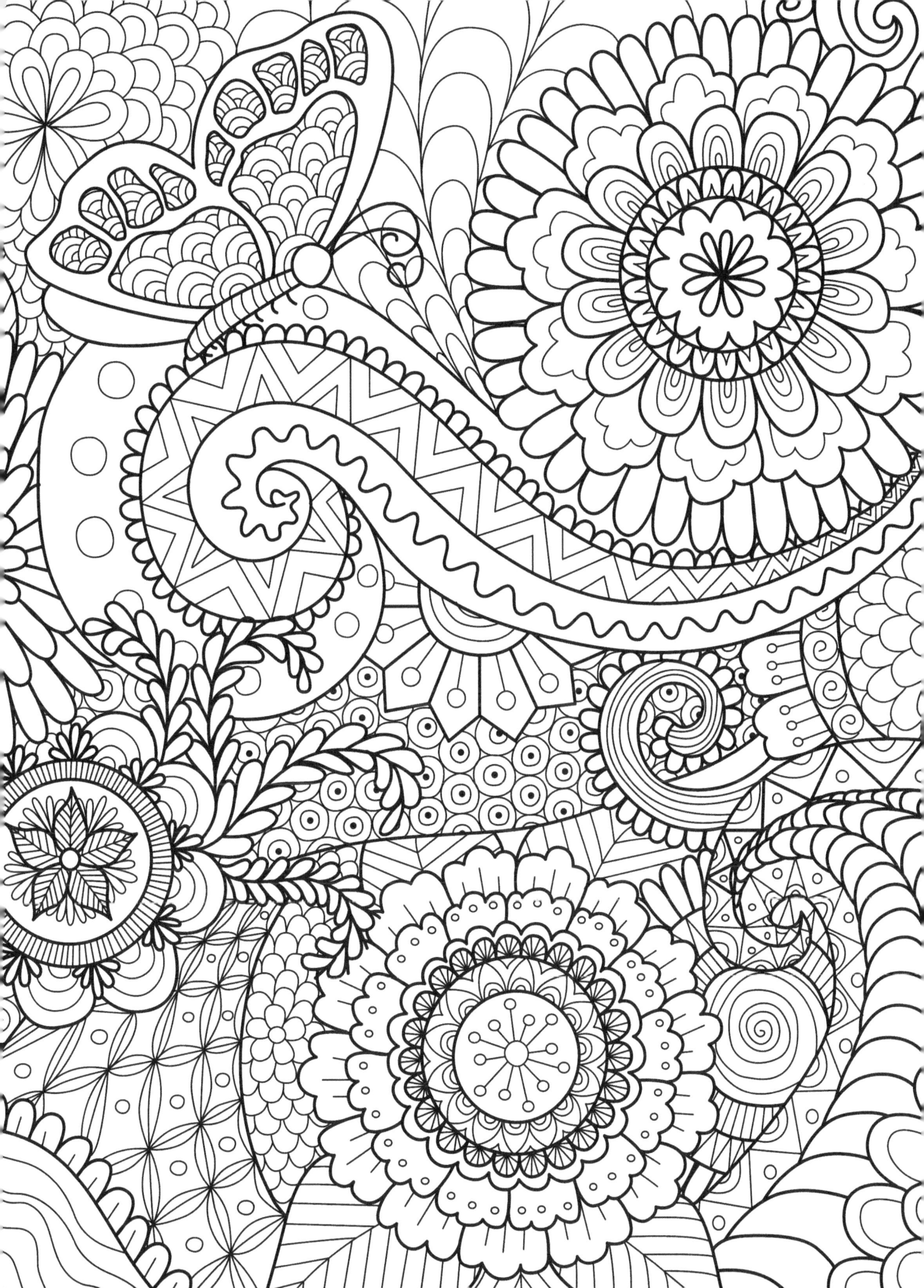

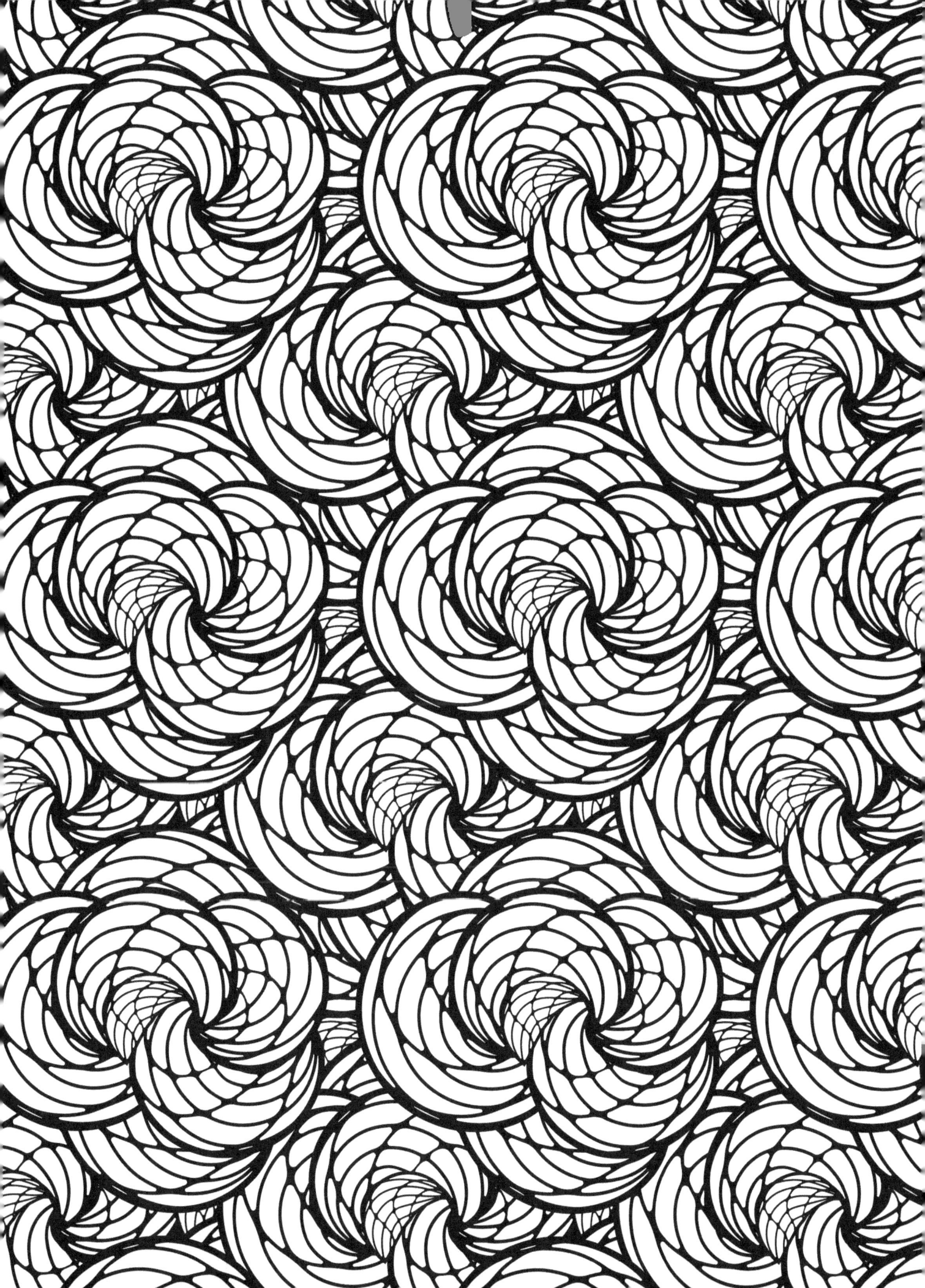

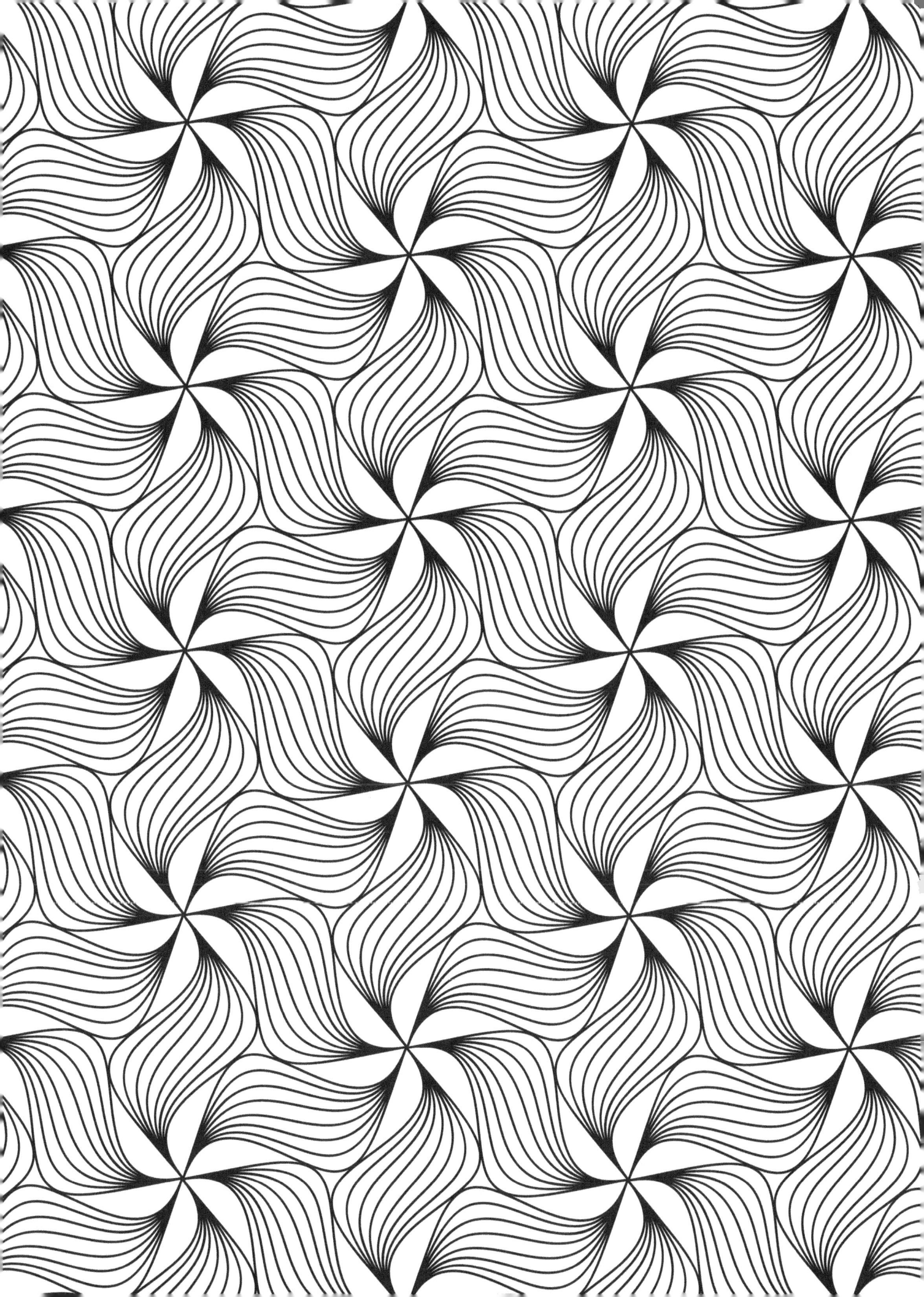

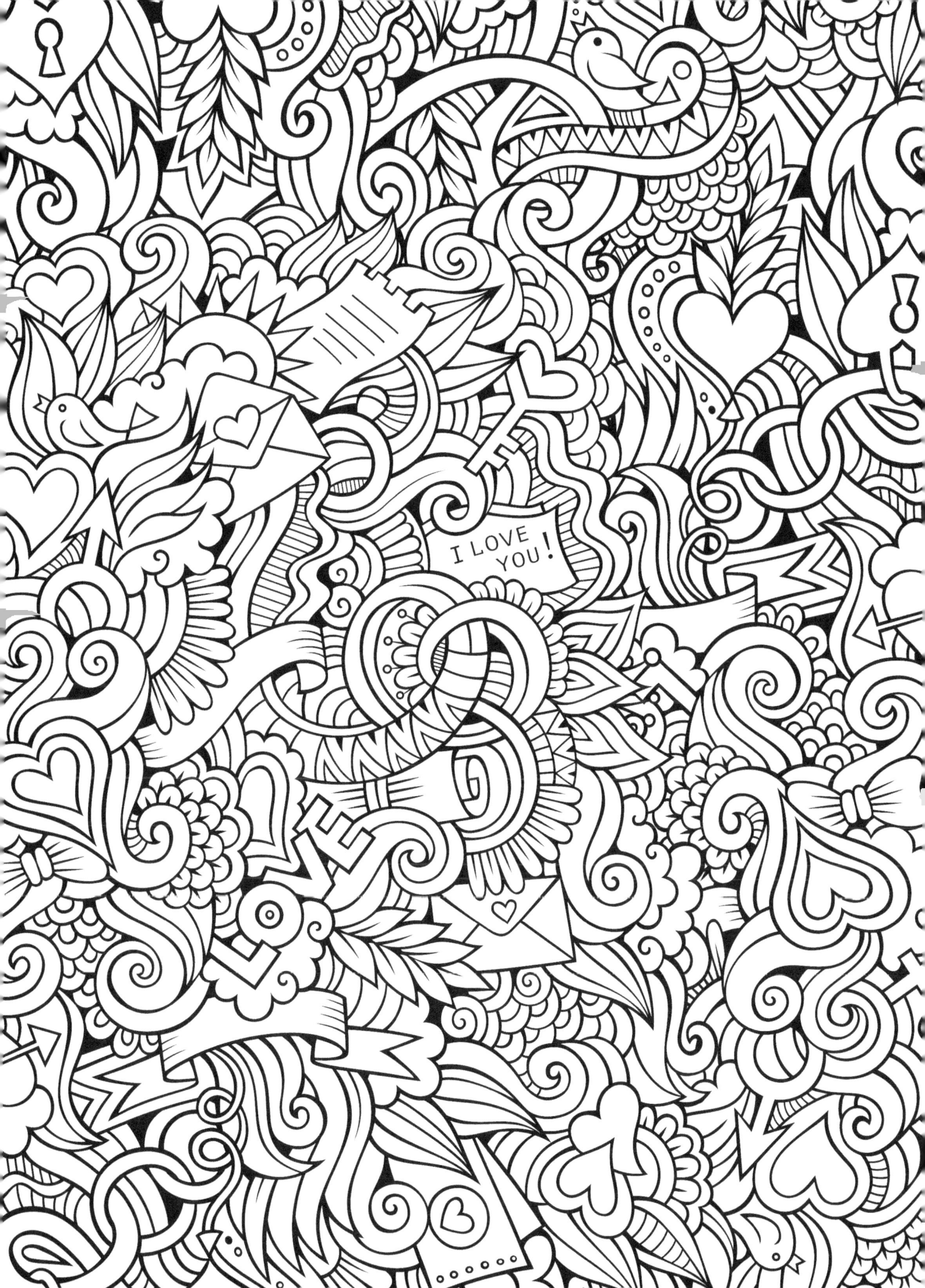

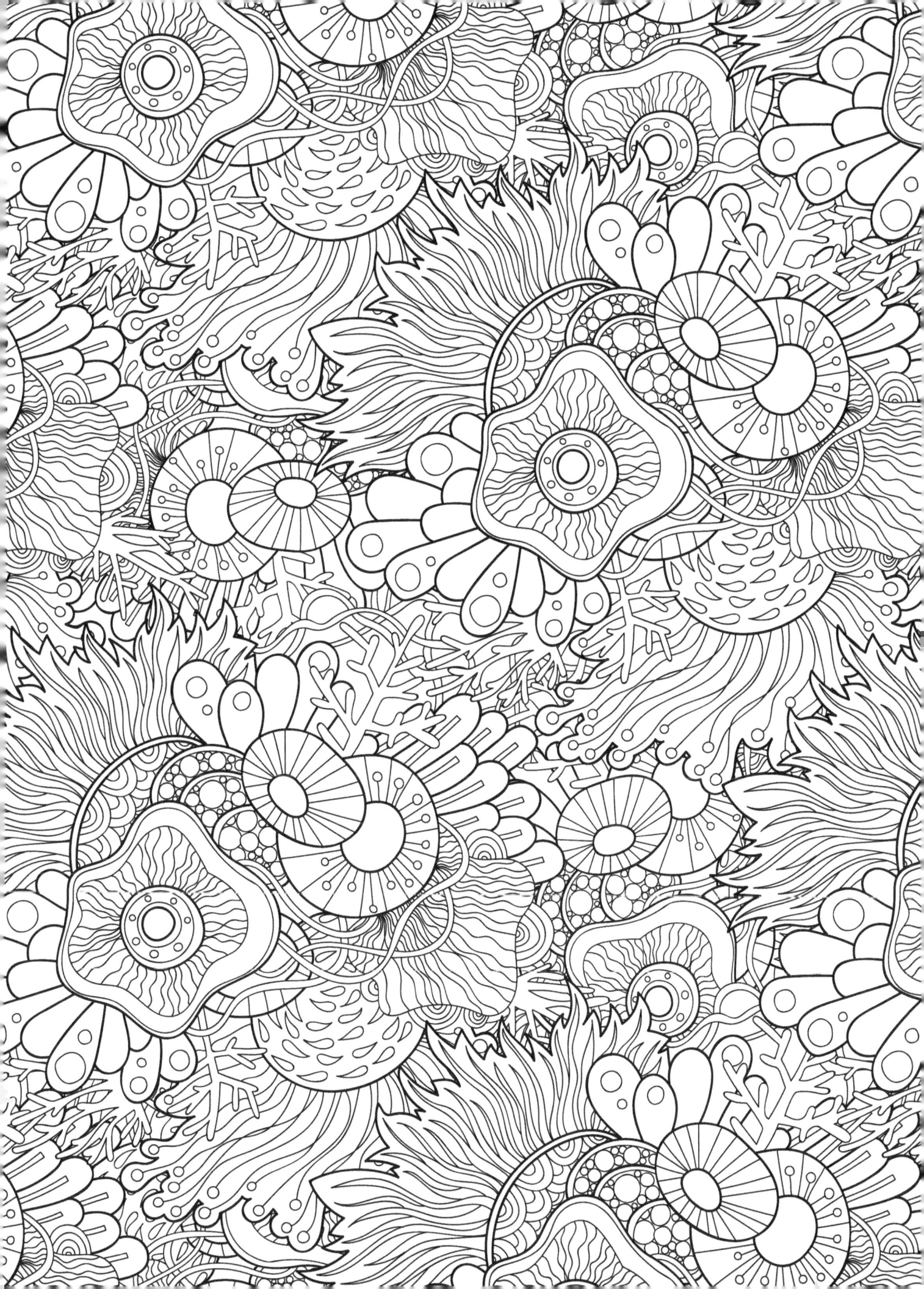

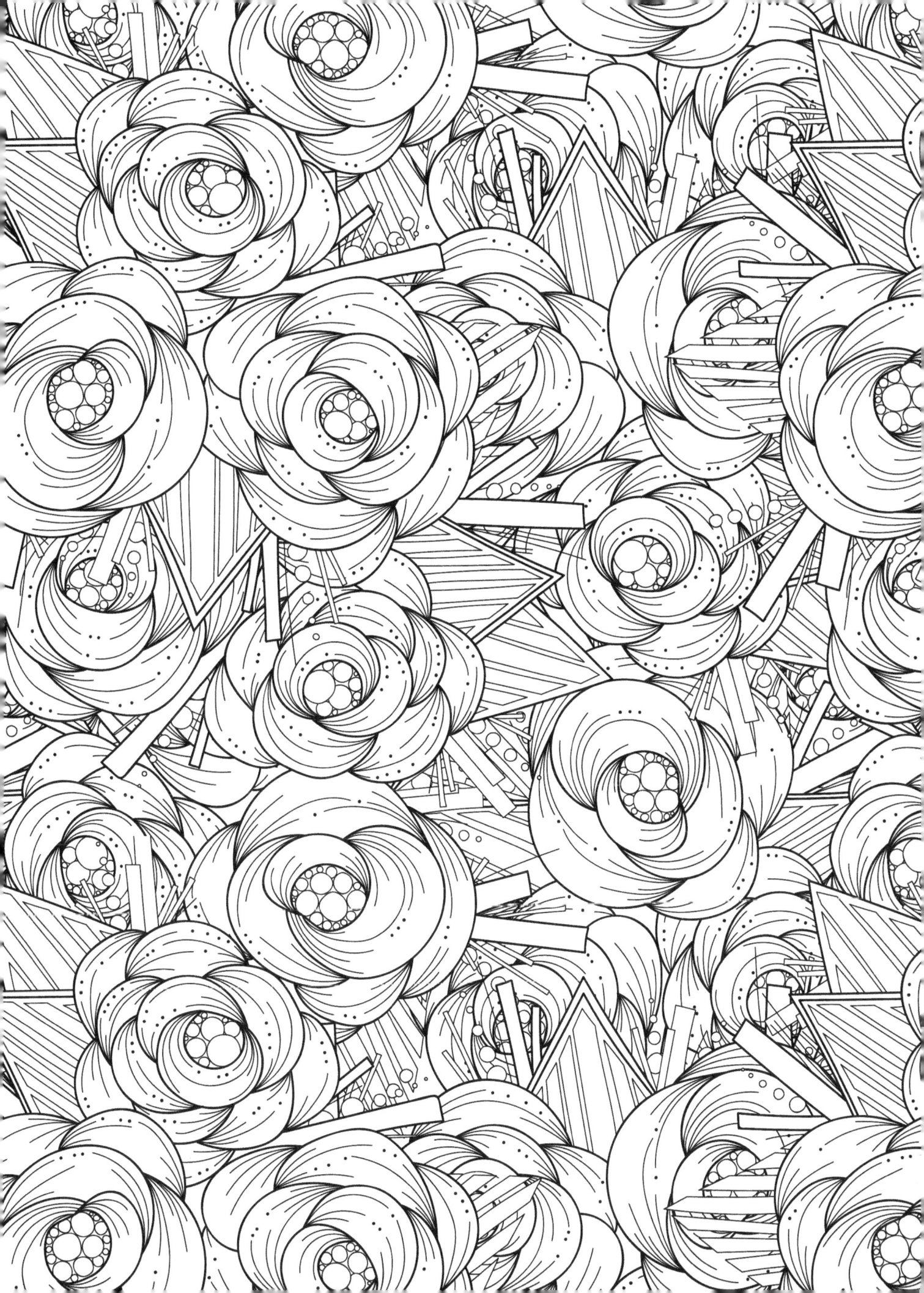

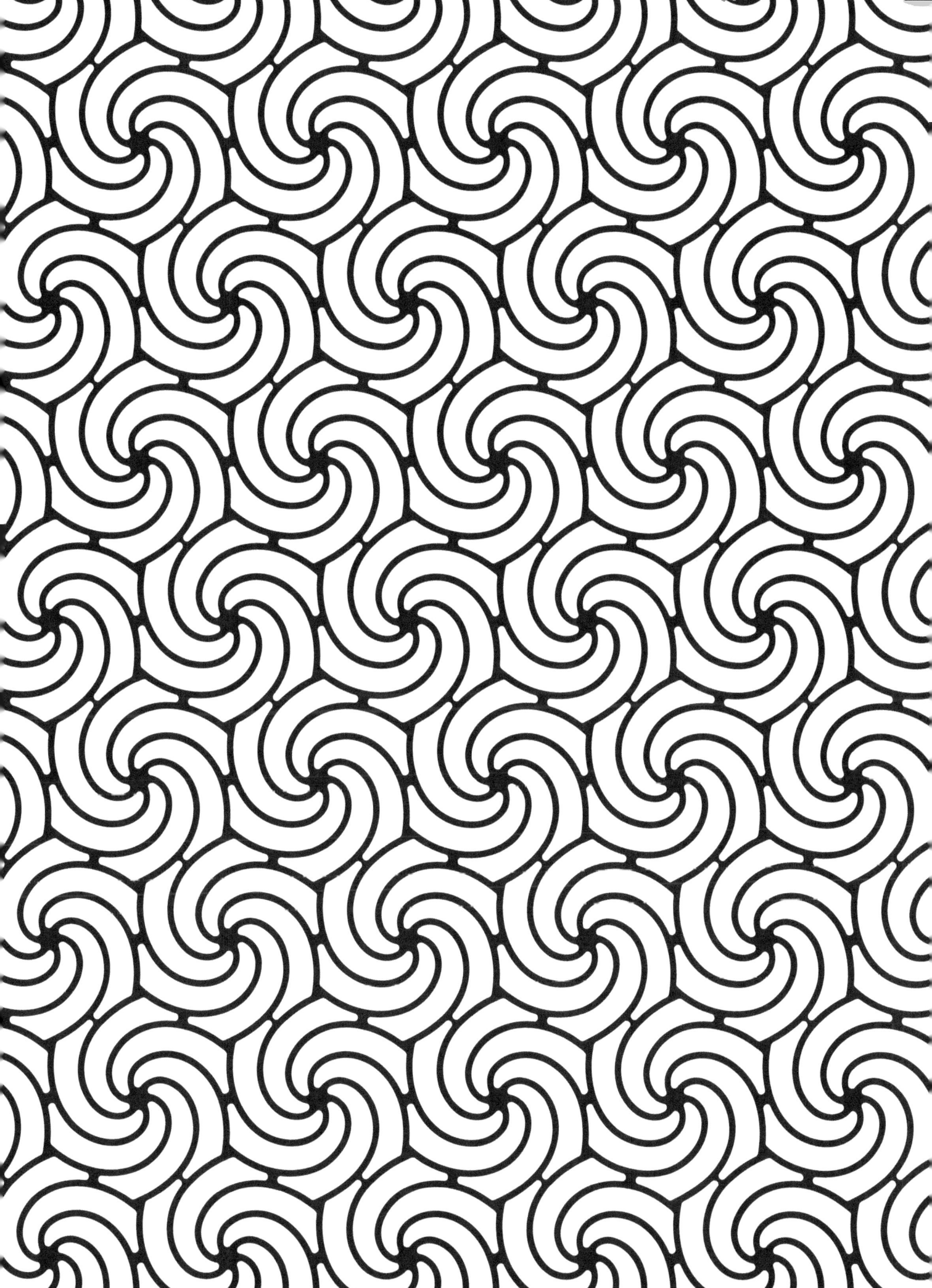

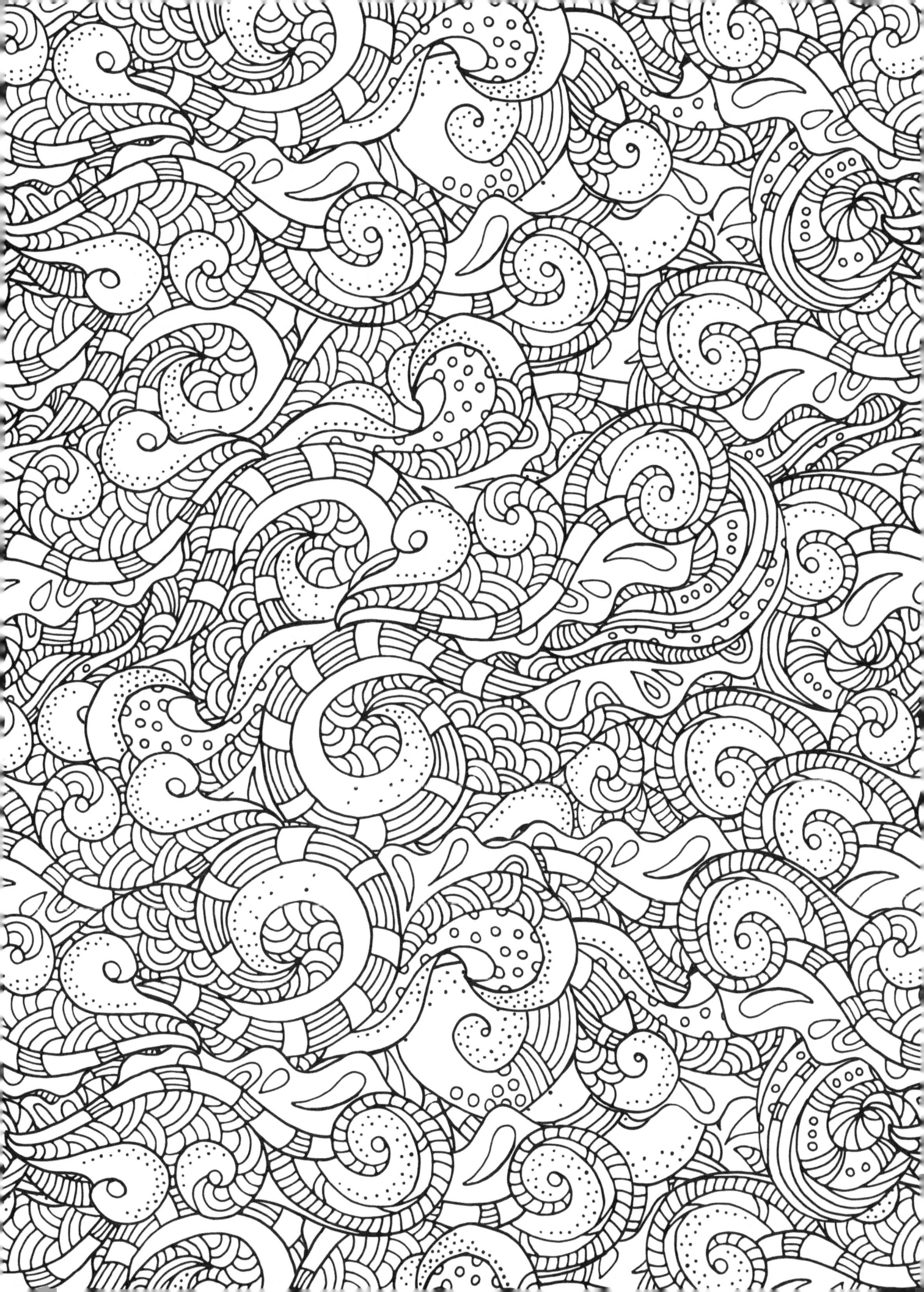

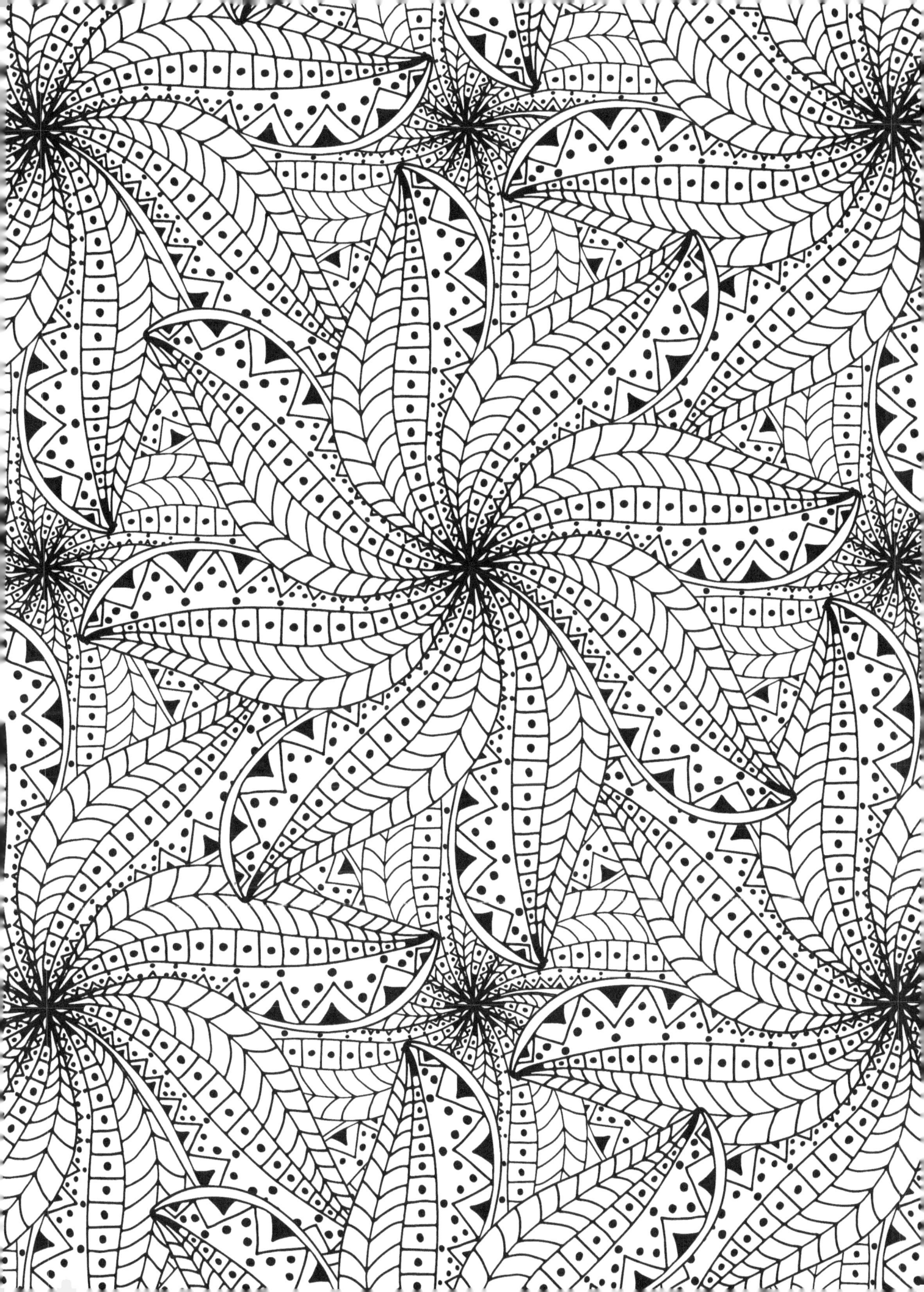

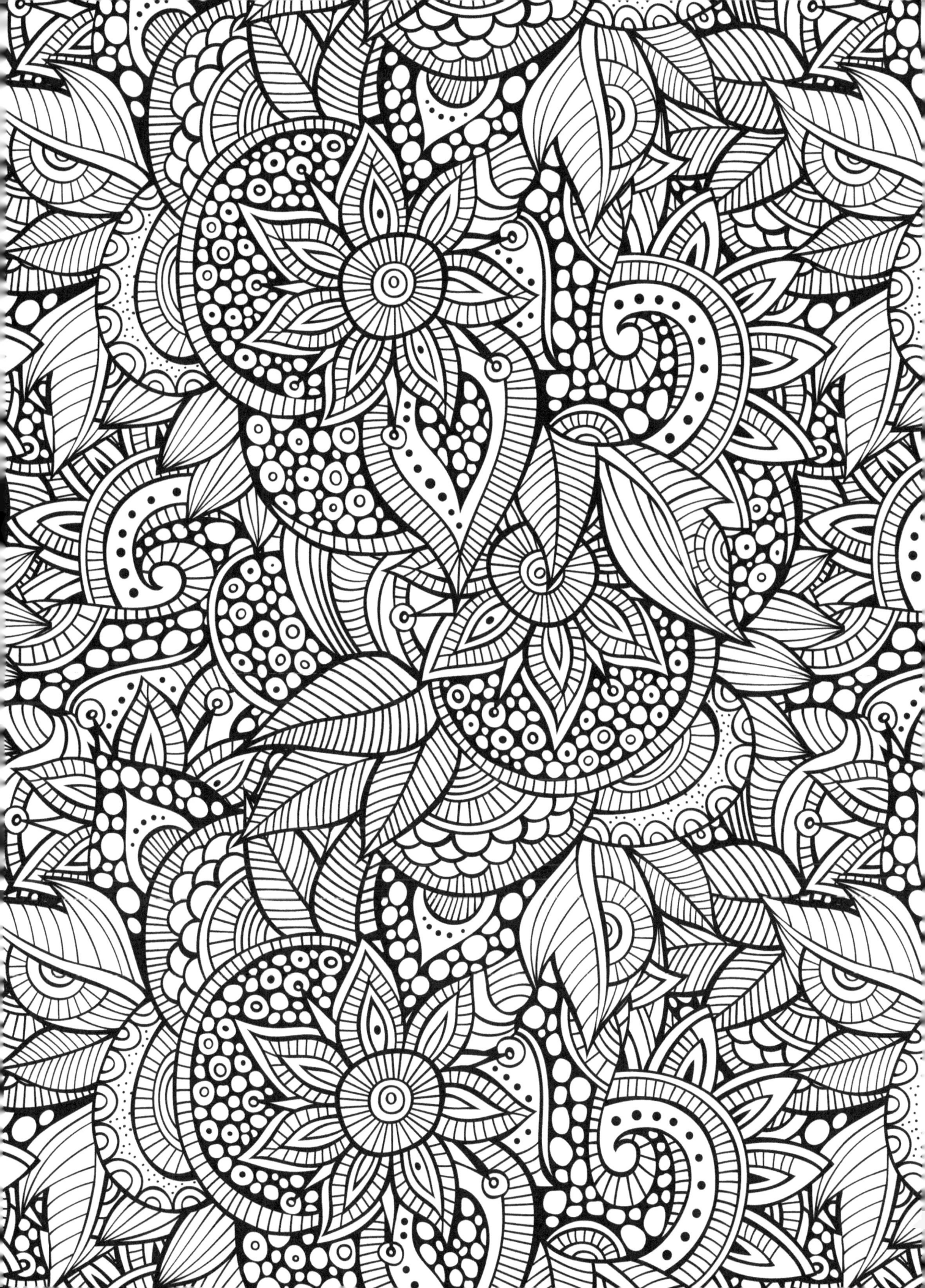

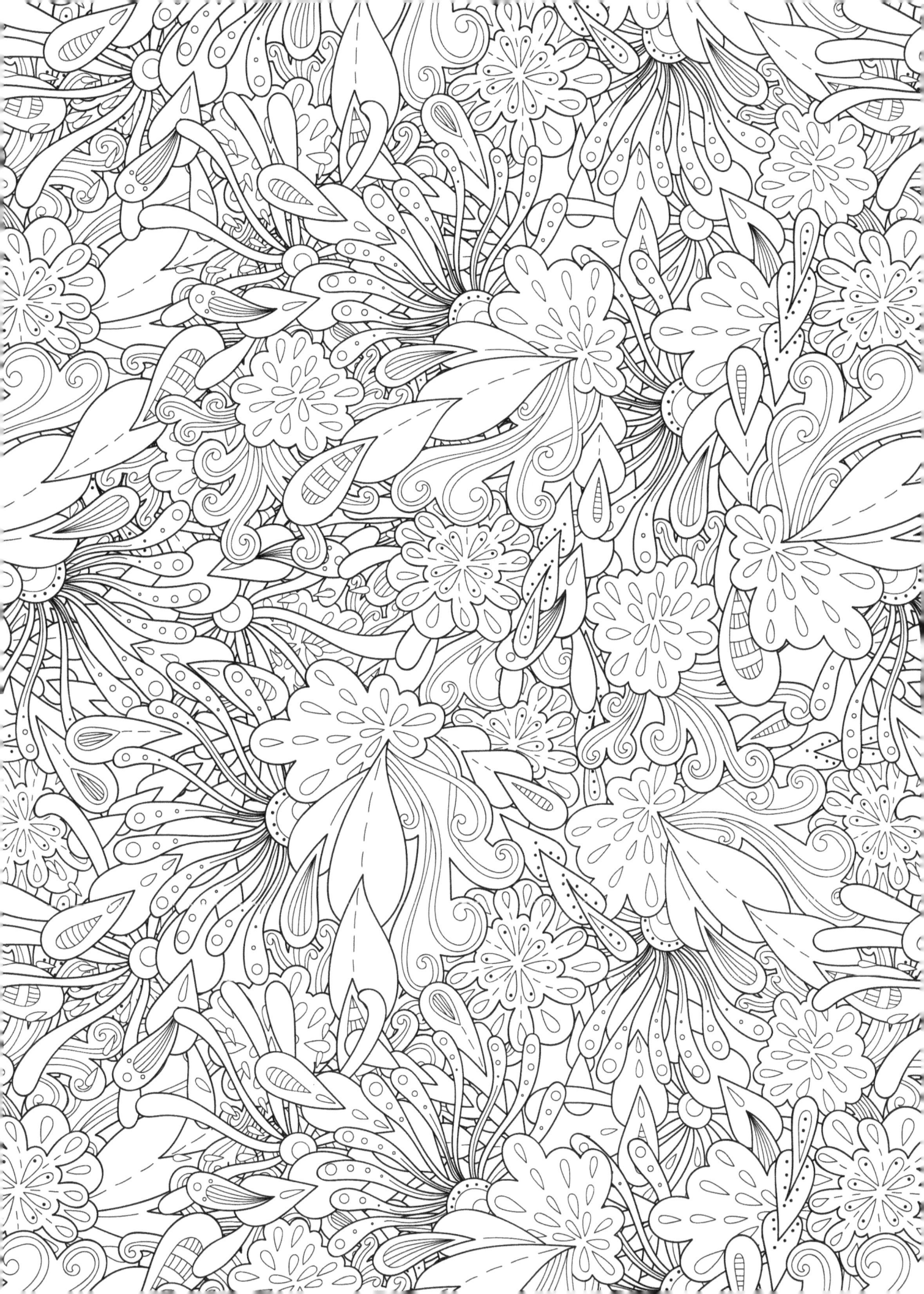

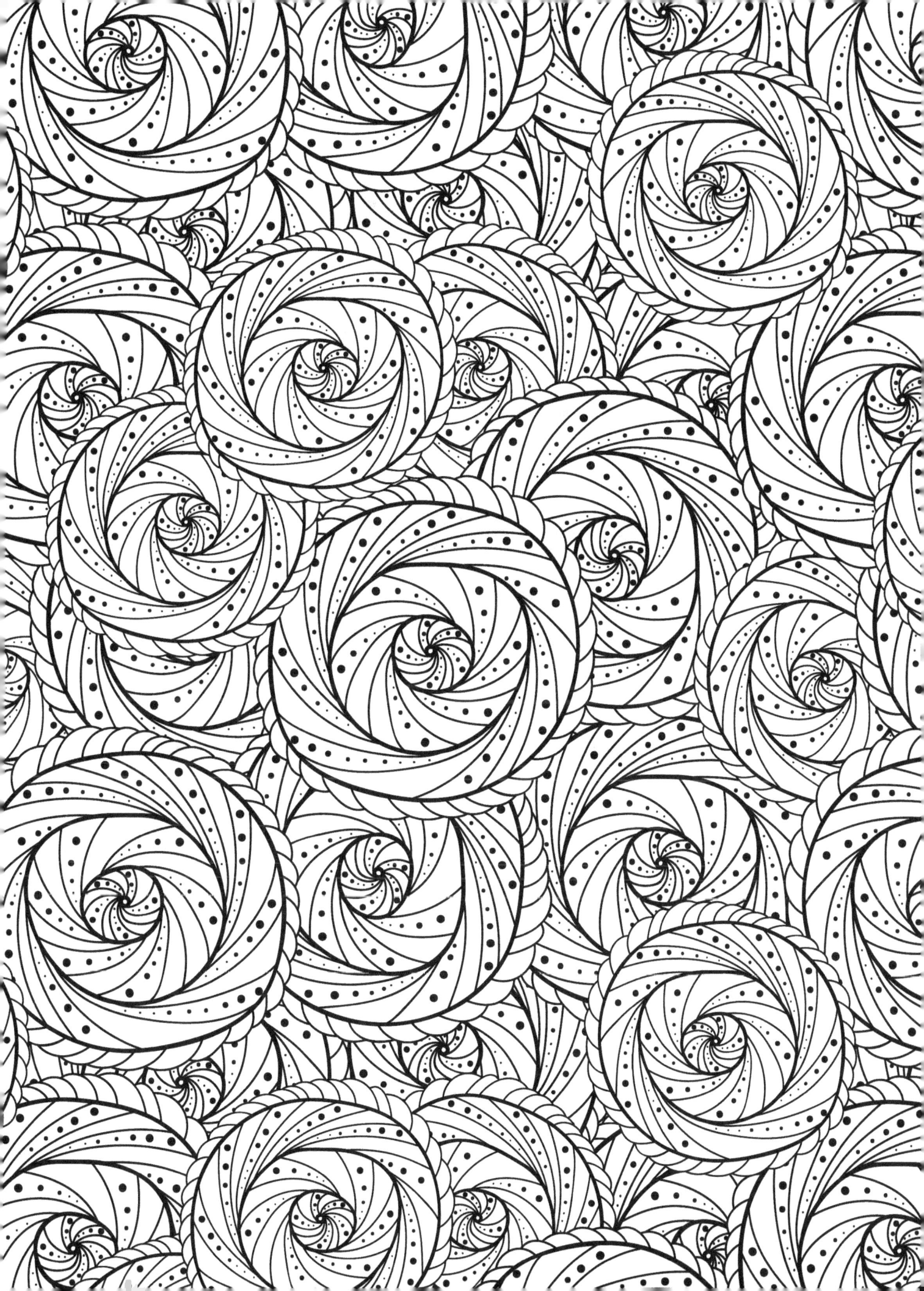

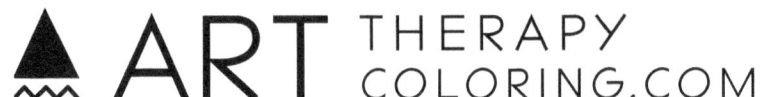

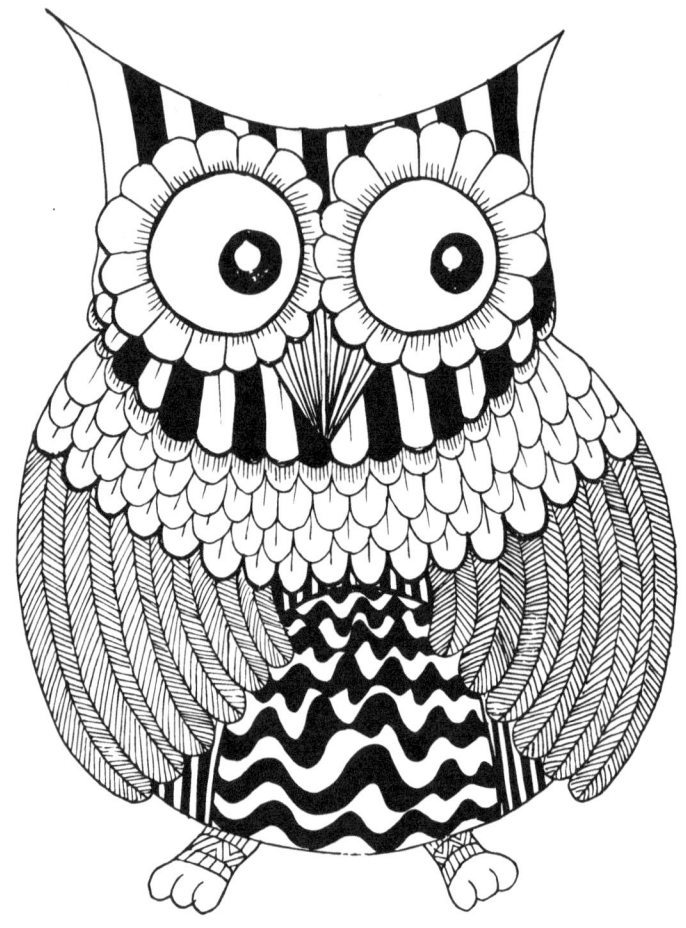

# Visit our website at www.arttherapycoloring.com

## Get a Free Printable Coloring Ebook!

We've created an exclusive offer for our customers to receive a free Adult Coloring Ebook.

Visit **www.arttherapycoloring.com/freebie** to claim your free coloring book with over 30 new designs that you can instantly print and color!

## Over 100 Art Therapy Coloring Books

See our collection of over 100 Art Therapy Coloring Books for Adults, Men, Seniors, Teens, Kids, Boys, and Girls on the following pages.

# Coloring Books For Adults

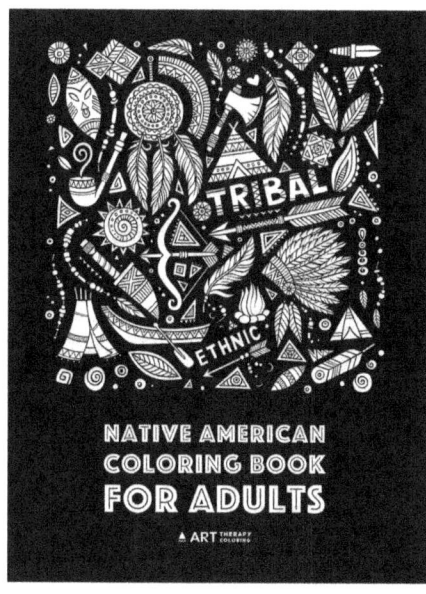

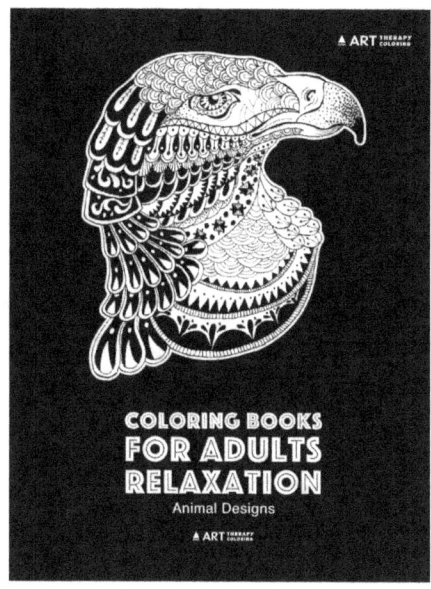

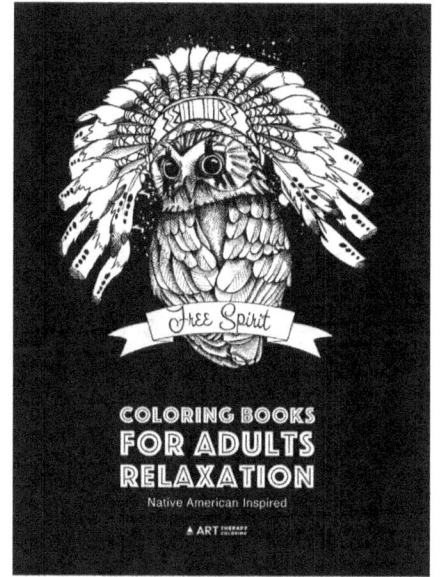

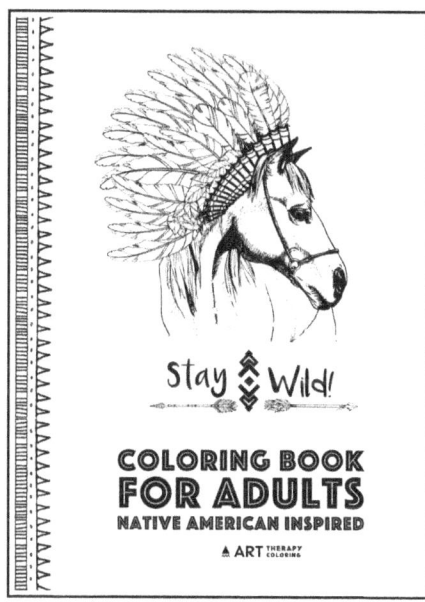

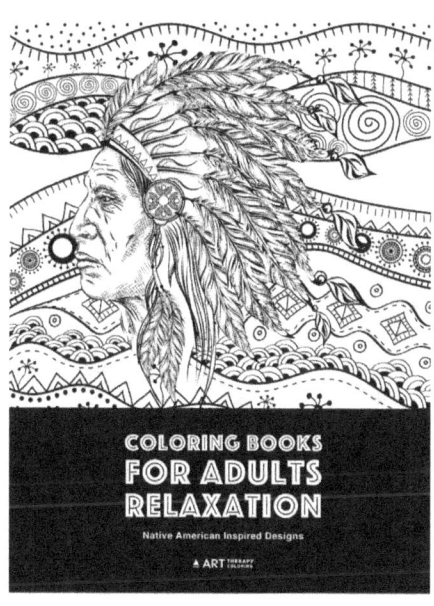

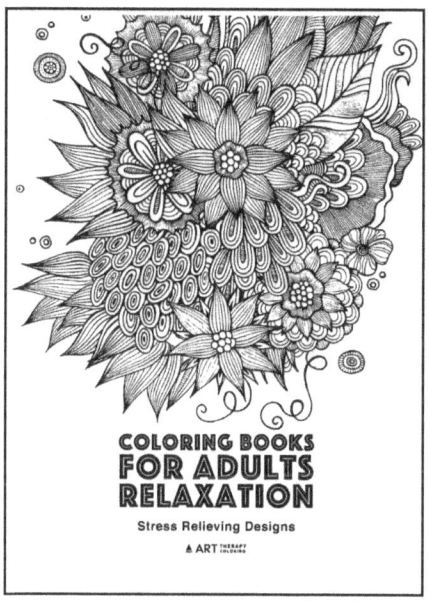

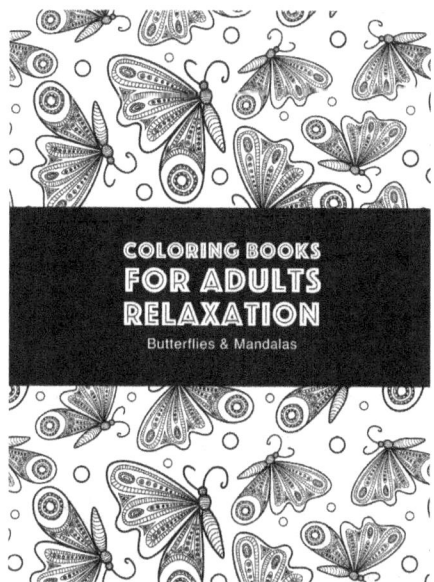

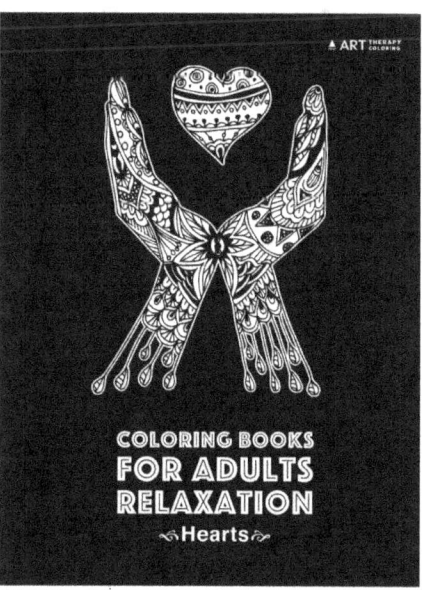

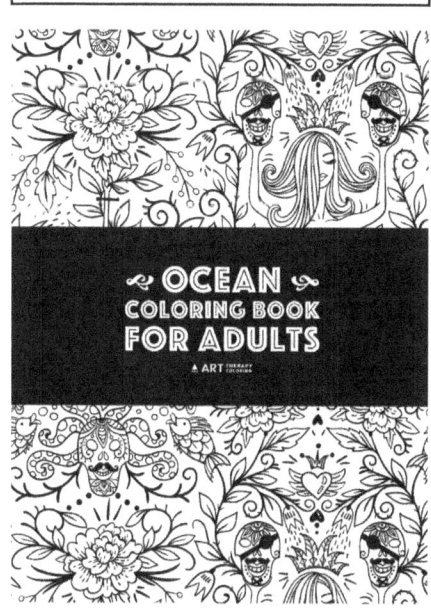

# Coloring Books For Adults

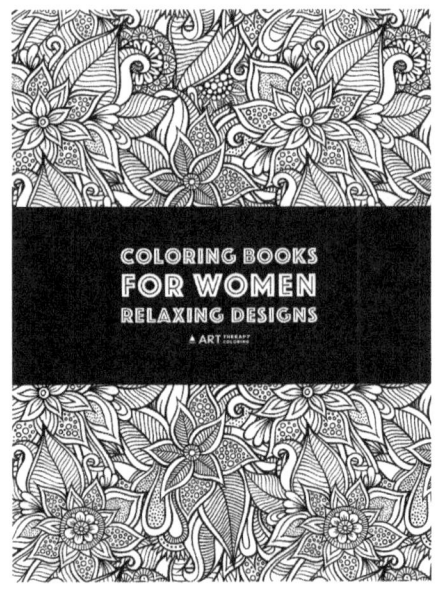

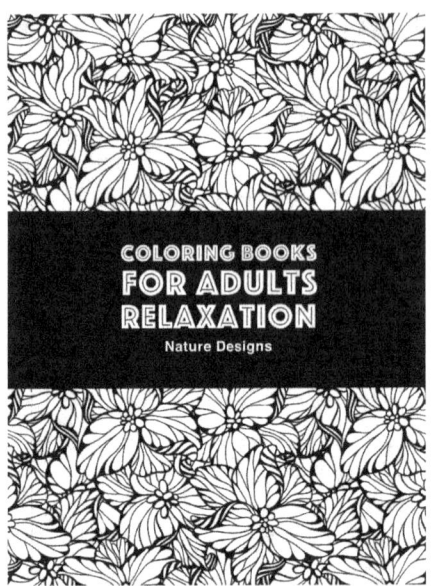

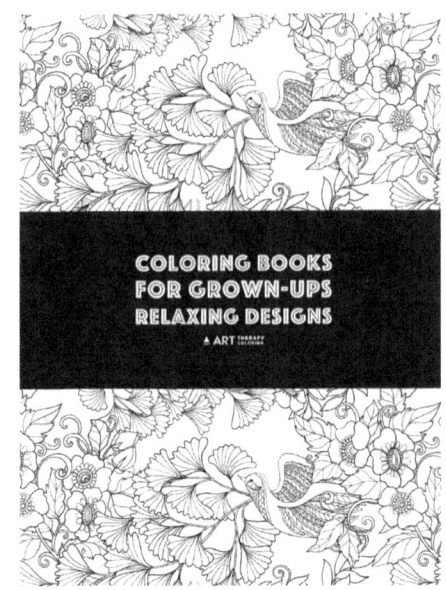

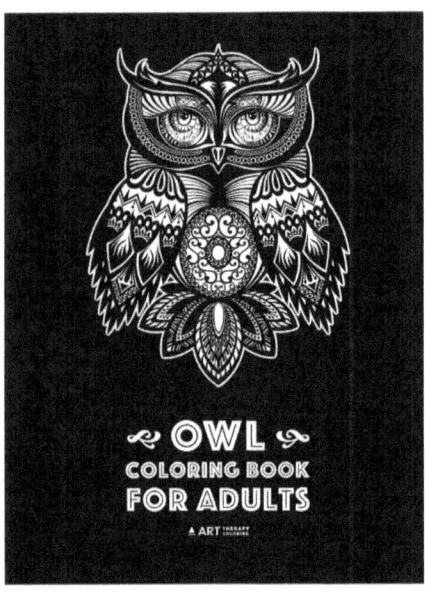

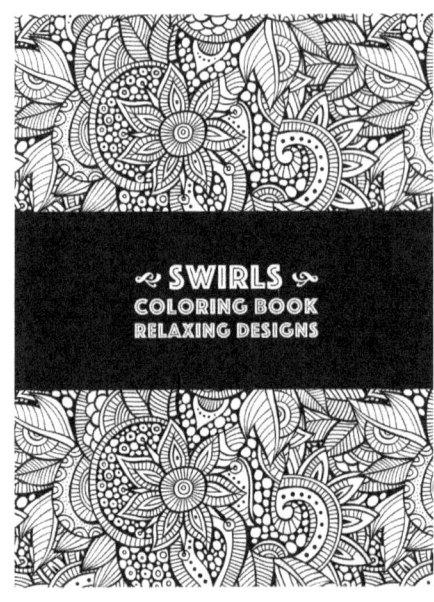

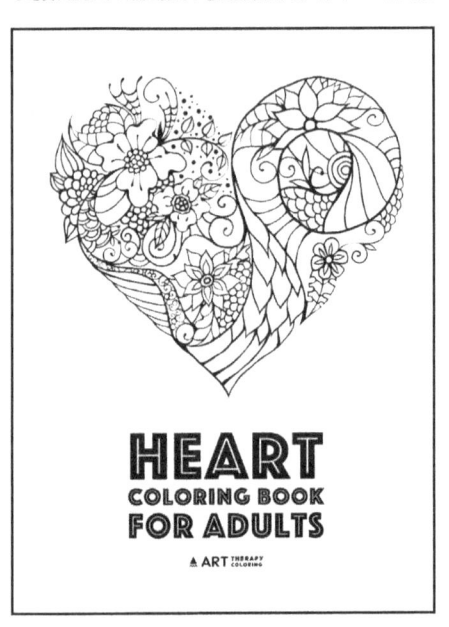

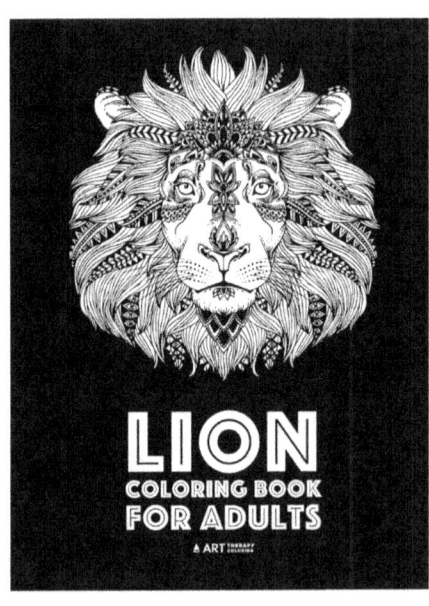

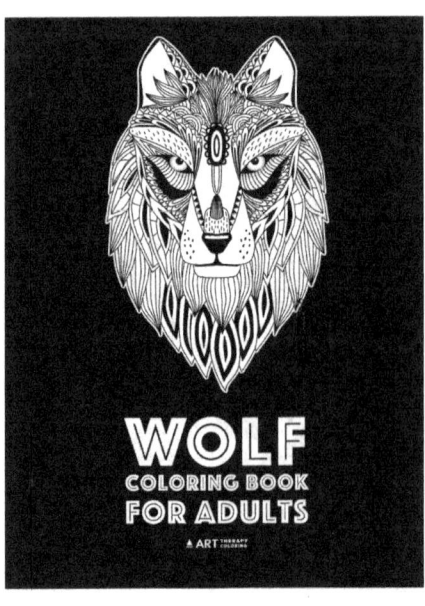

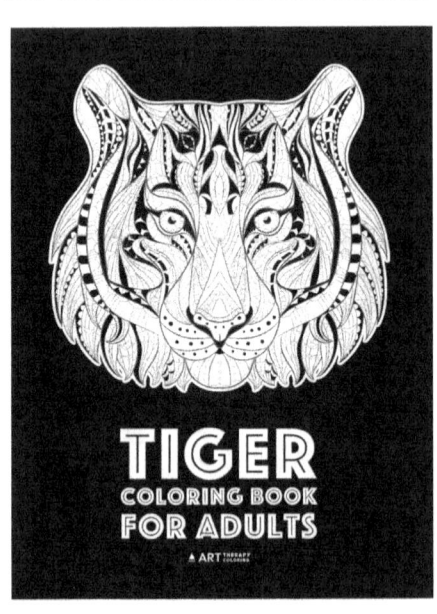

# Coloring Books For Men

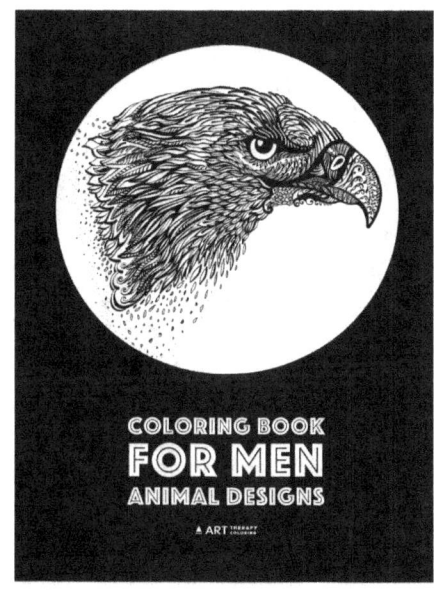

COLORING BOOK
**FOR MEN**
ANIMAL DESIGNS

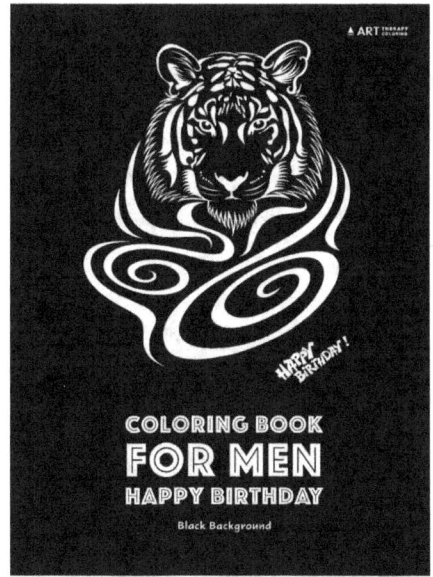

HAPPY
BIRTHDAY!

COLORING BOOK
**FOR MEN**
HAPPY BIRTHDAY

Black Background

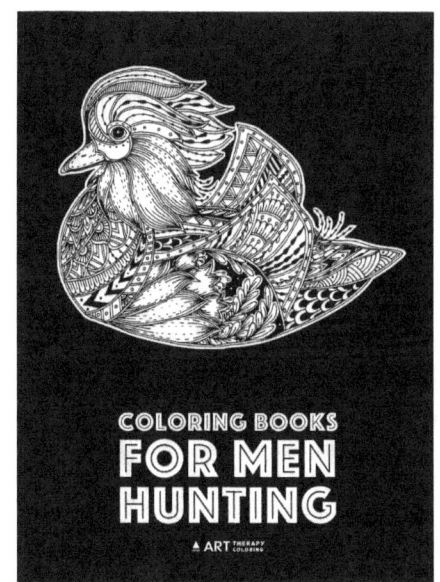

COLORING BOOKS
**FOR MEN**
HUNTING

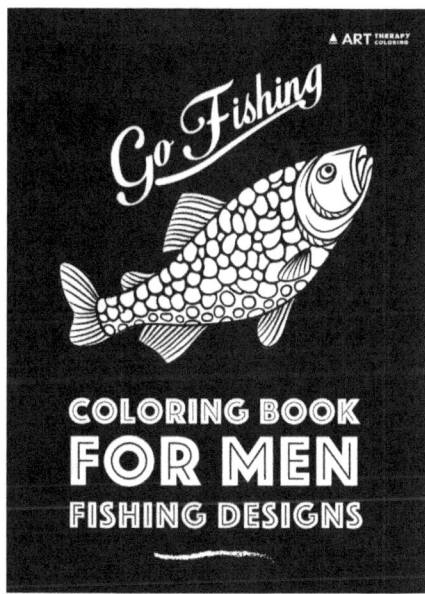

Go Fishing

COLORING BOOK
**FOR MEN**
FISHING DESIGNS

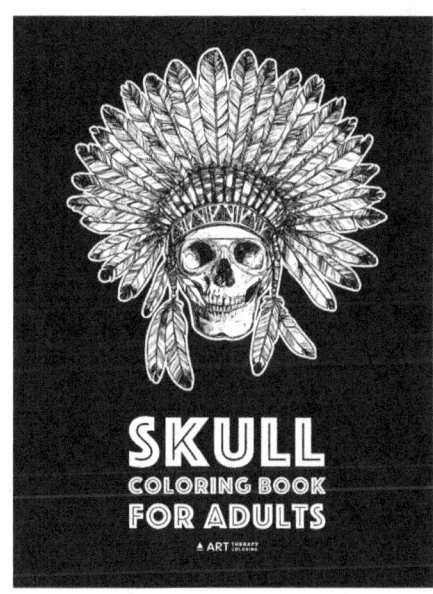

**SKULL**
COLORING BOOK
FOR ADULTS

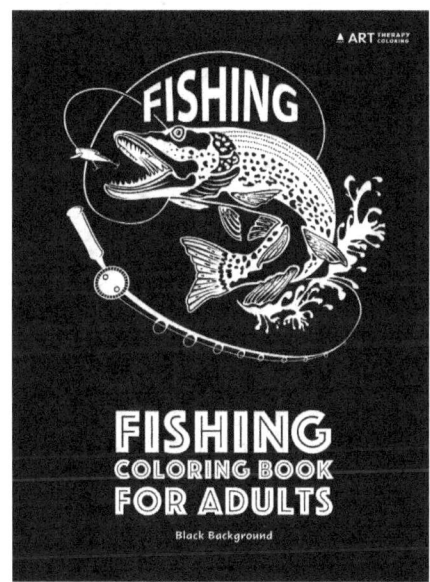

FISHING

**FISHING**
COLORING BOOK
FOR ADULTS

Black Background

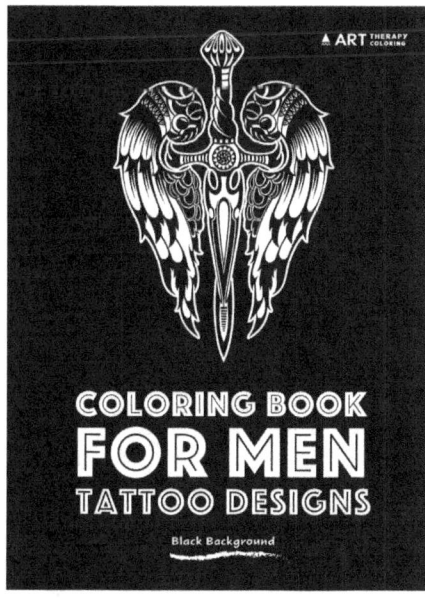

COLORING BOOK
**FOR MEN**
TATTOO DESIGNS

Black Background

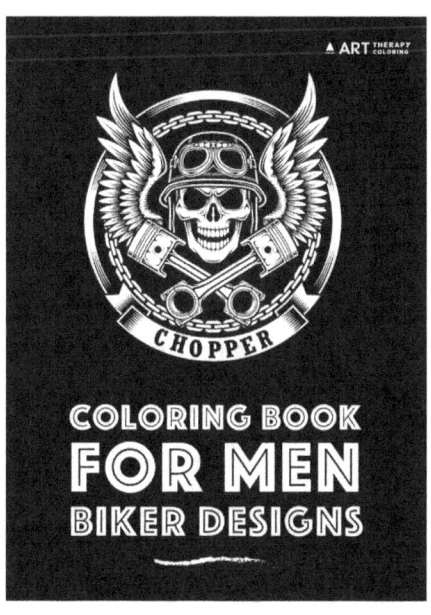

CHOPPER

COLORING BOOK
**FOR MEN**
BIKER DESIGNS

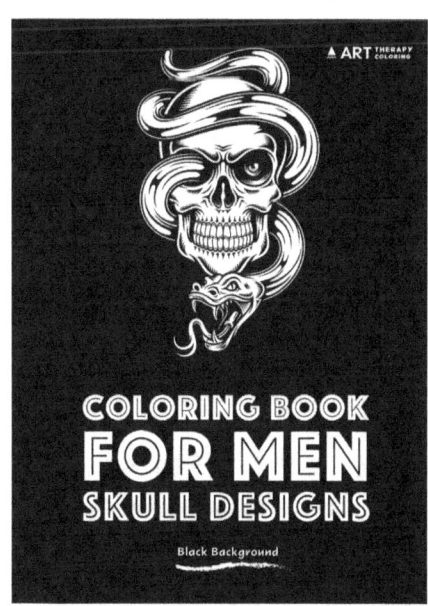

COLORING BOOK
**FOR MEN**
SKULL DESIGNS

Black Background

# Coloring Books For Seniors

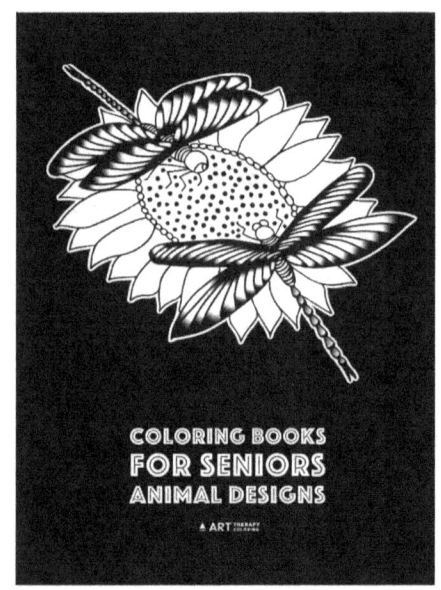

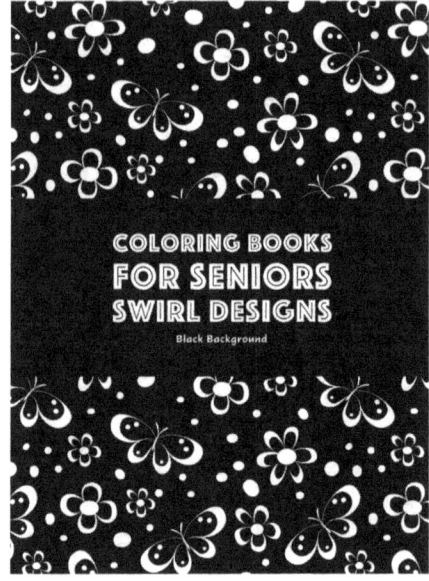

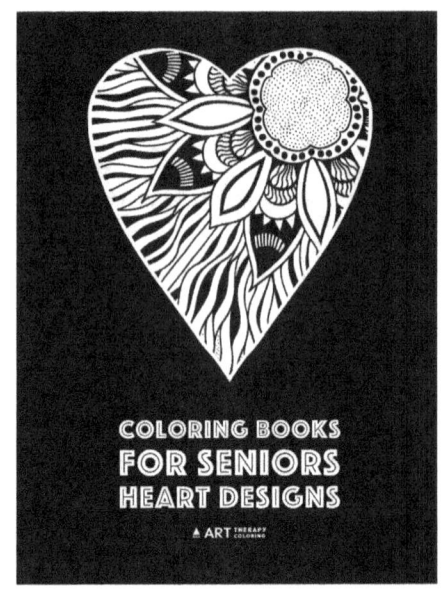

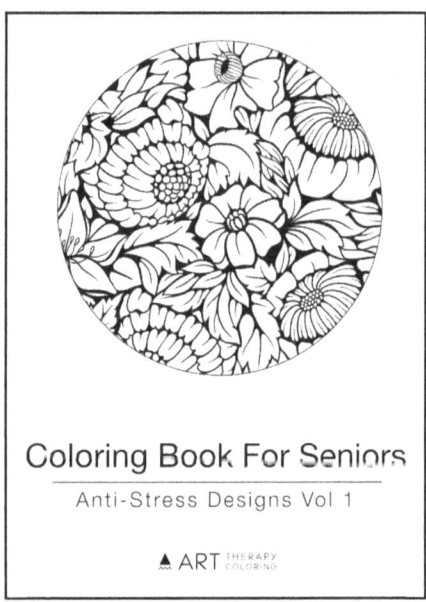

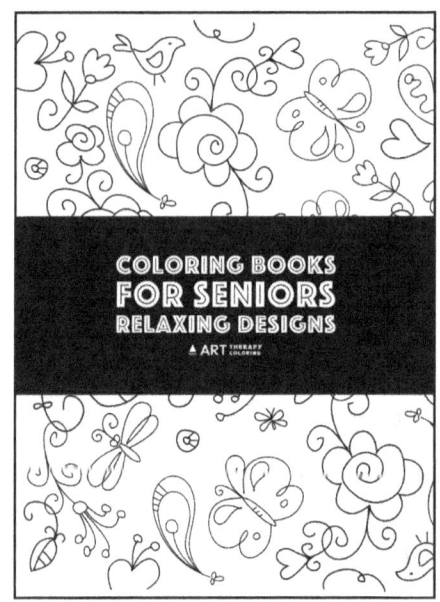

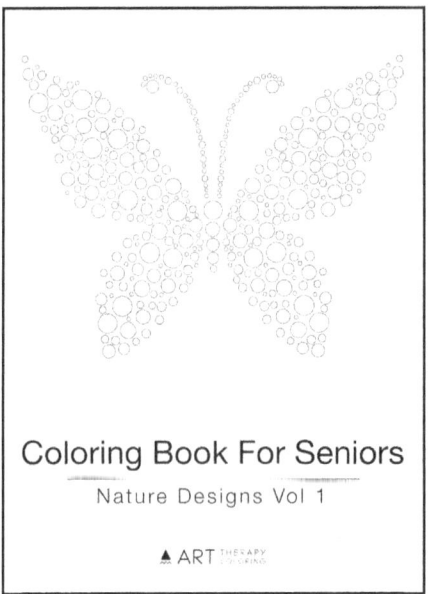

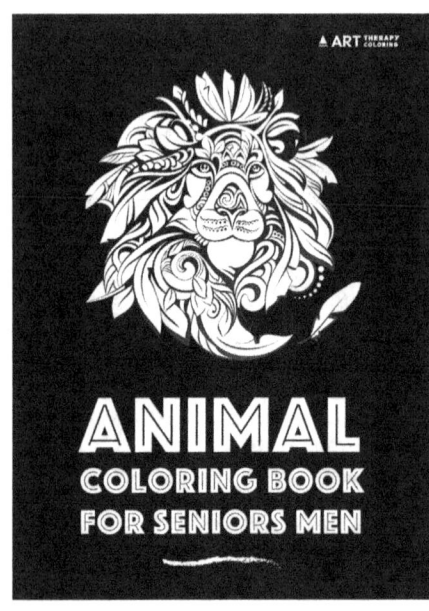

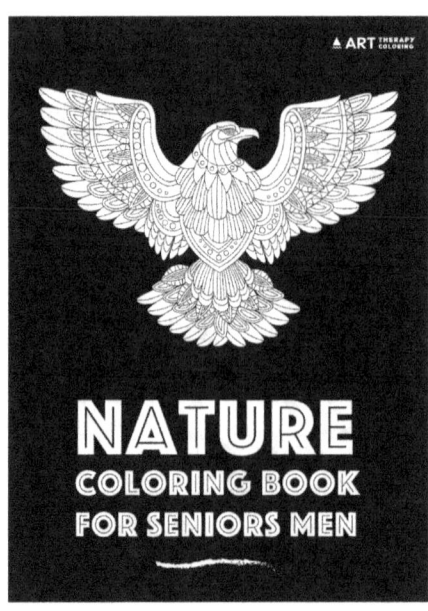

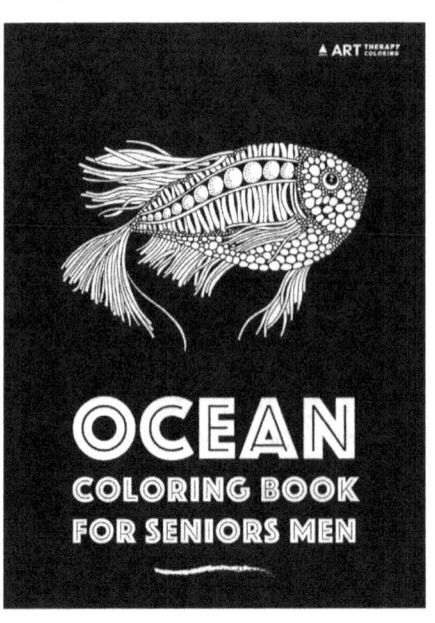

# Coloring Books For Girls

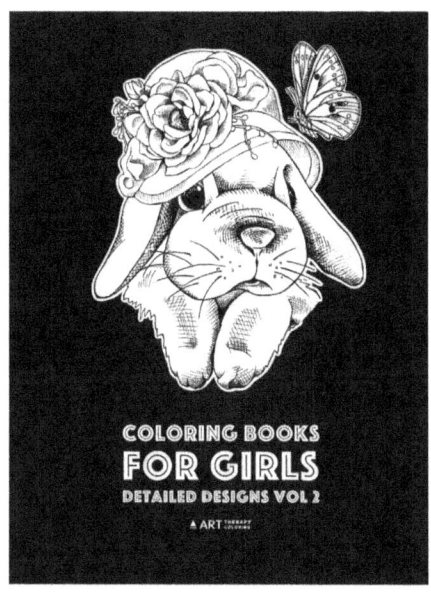

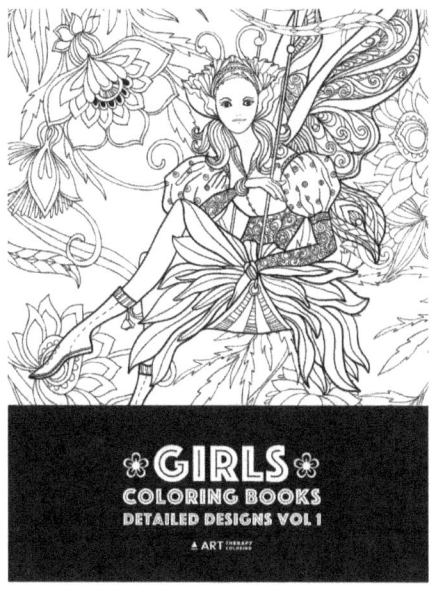

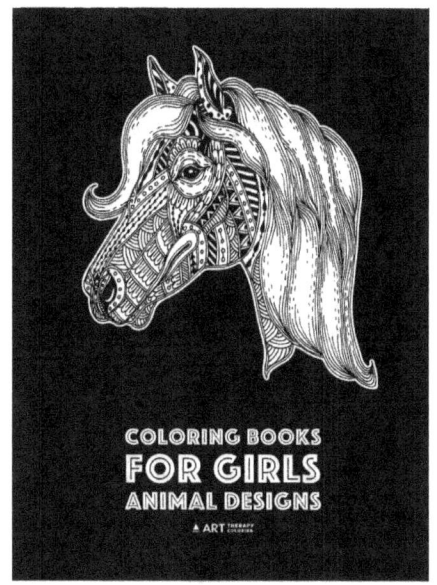

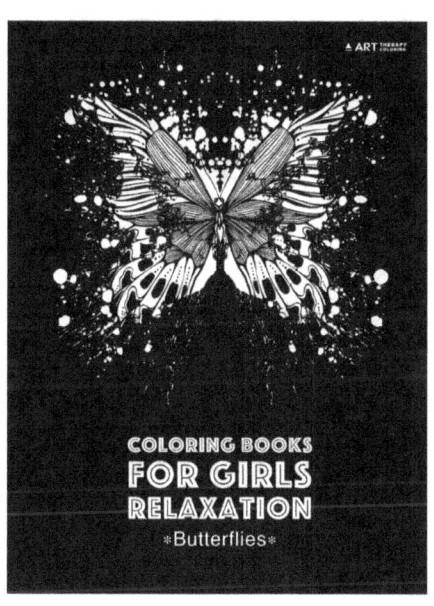

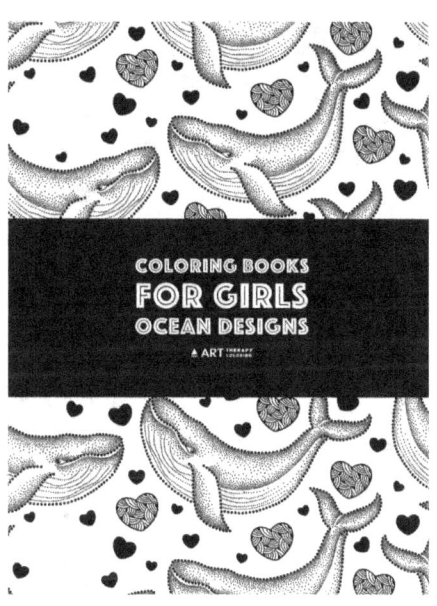

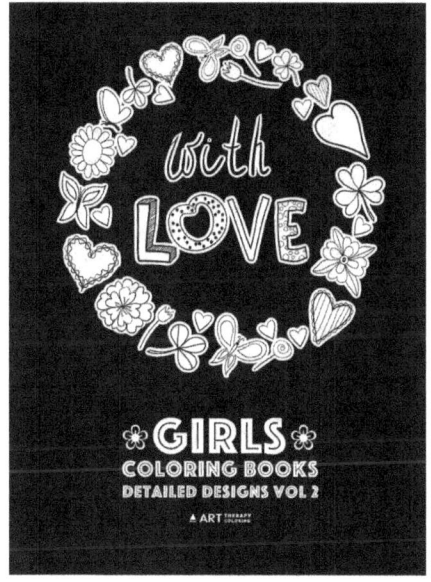

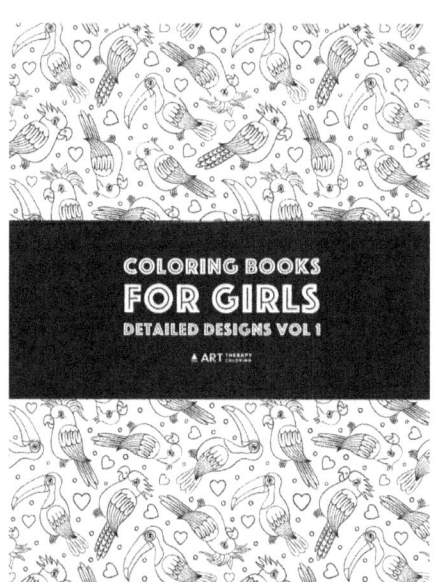

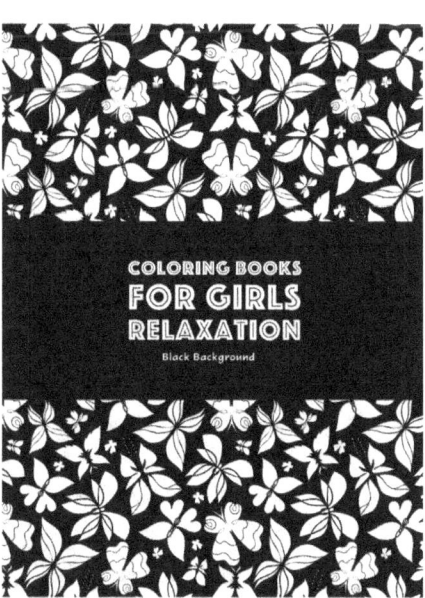

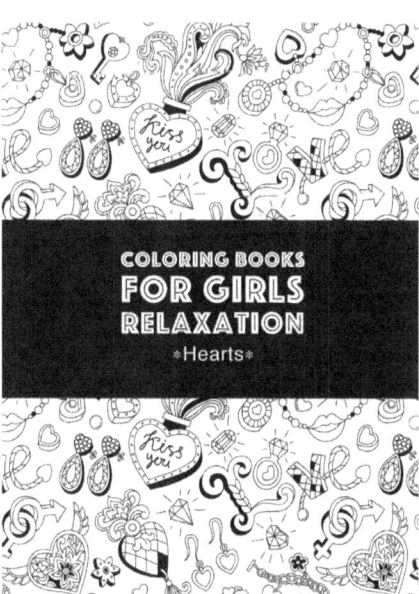

# Coloring Books For Boys

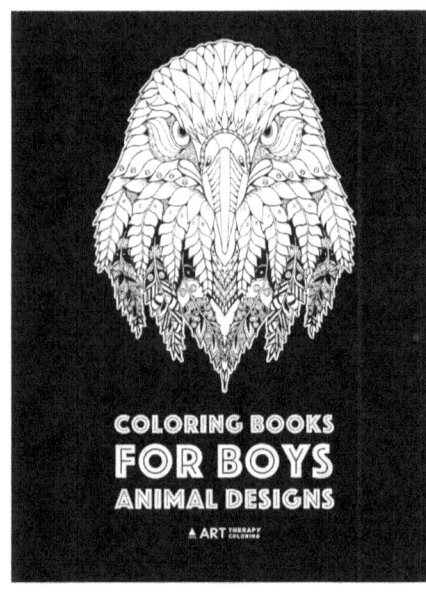

COLORING BOOKS
**FOR BOYS**
ANIMAL DESIGNS
ART THERAPY COLORING

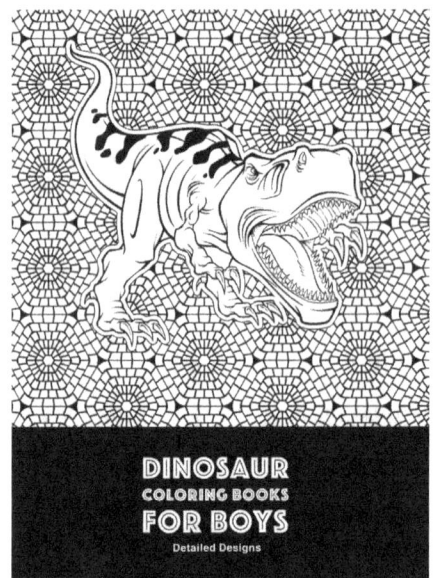

**DINOSAUR**
COLORING BOOKS
**FOR BOYS**
Detailed Designs

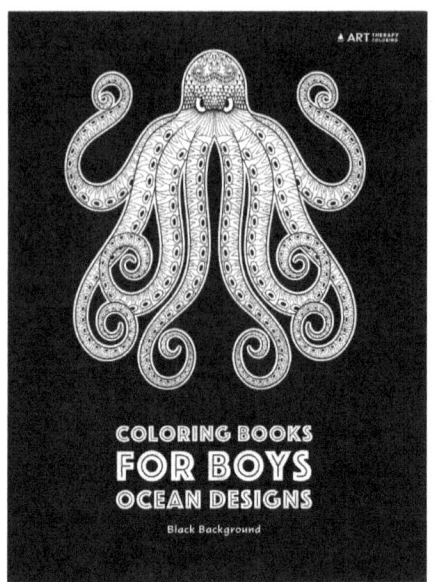

COLORING BOOKS
**FOR BOYS**
OCEAN DESIGNS
Black Background

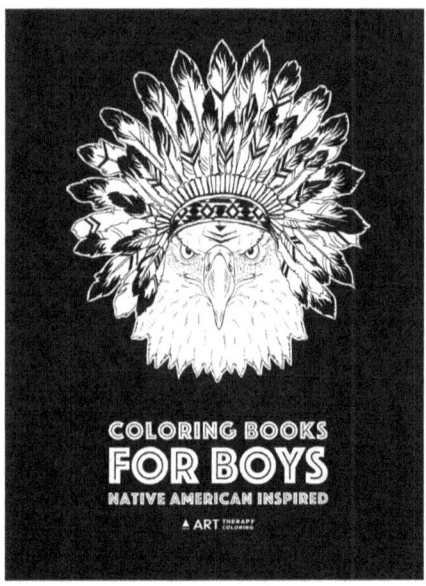

COLORING BOOKS
**FOR BOYS**
NATIVE AMERICAN INSPIRED
ART THERAPY COLORING

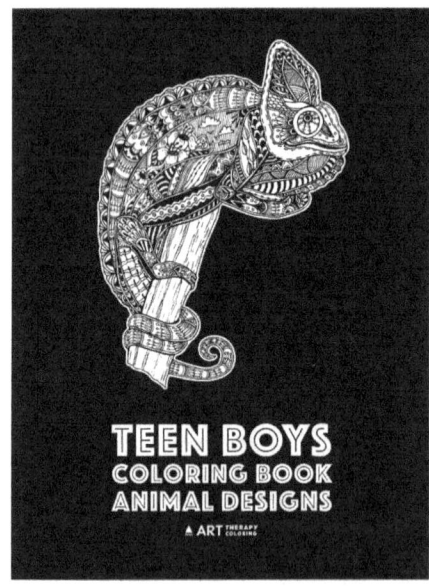

**TEEN BOYS**
COLORING BOOK
ANIMAL DESIGNS
ART THERAPY COLORING

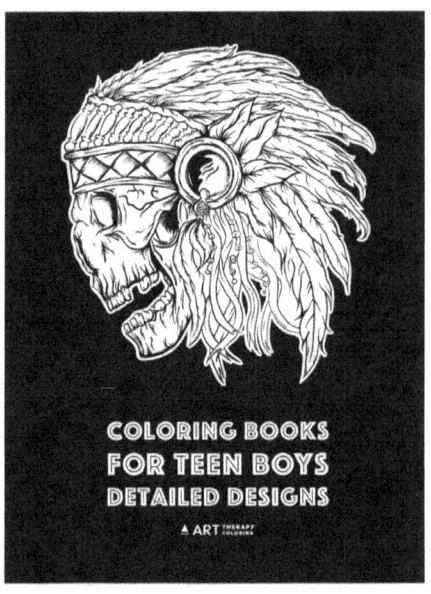

COLORING BOOKS
FOR TEEN BOYS
DETAILED DESIGNS
ART THERAPY COLORING

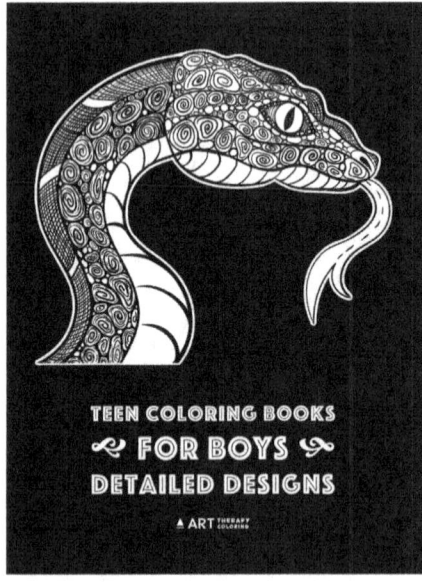

TEEN COLORING BOOKS
**FOR BOYS**
DETAILED DESIGNS
ART THERAPY COLORING

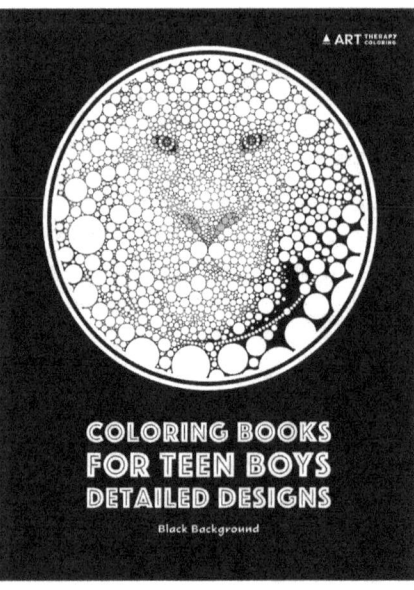

COLORING BOOKS
FOR TEEN BOYS
DETAILED DESIGNS
Black Background

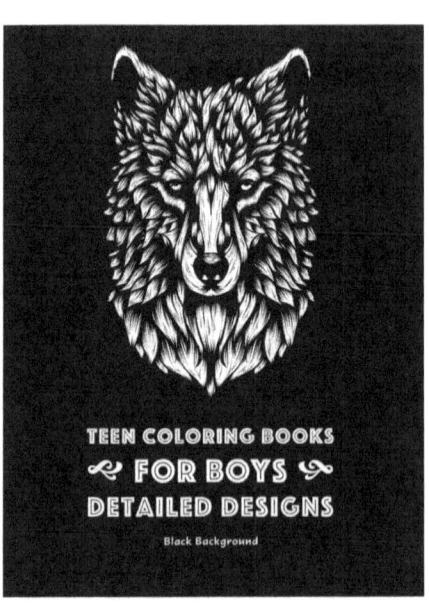

TEEN COLORING BOOKS
**FOR BOYS**
DETAILED DESIGNS
Black Background

# Coloring Books For Kids

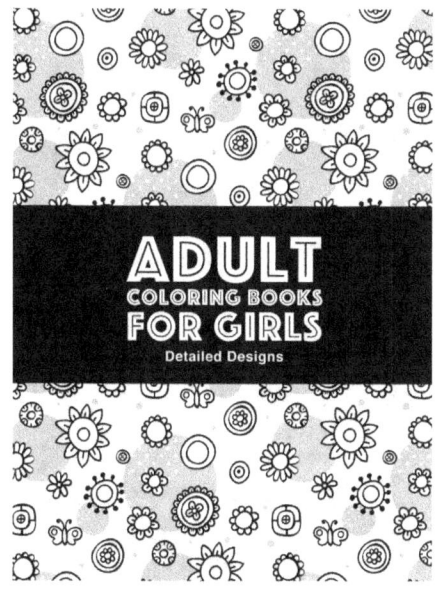

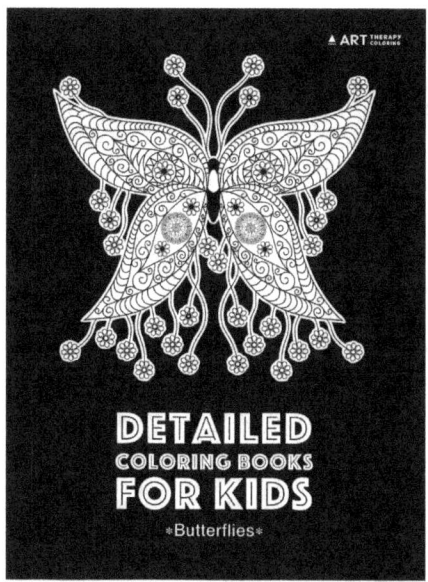

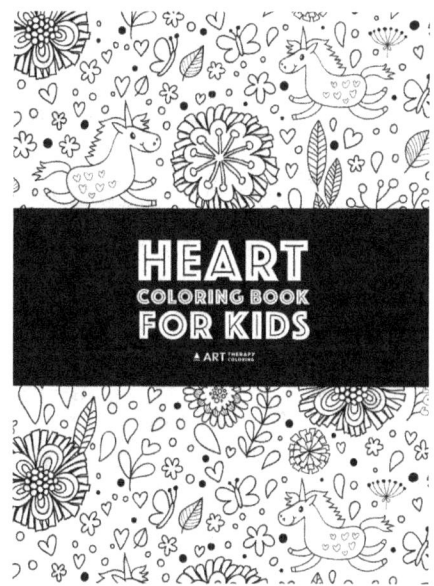

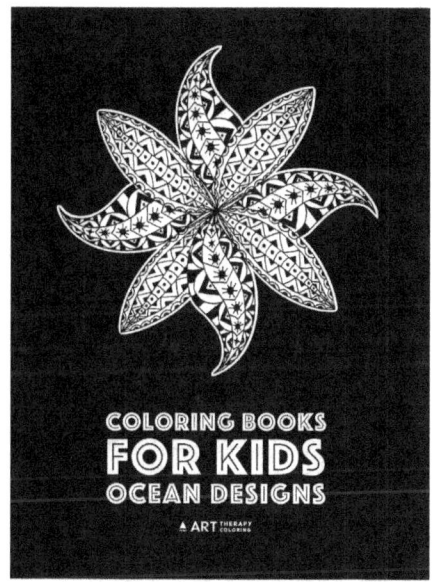

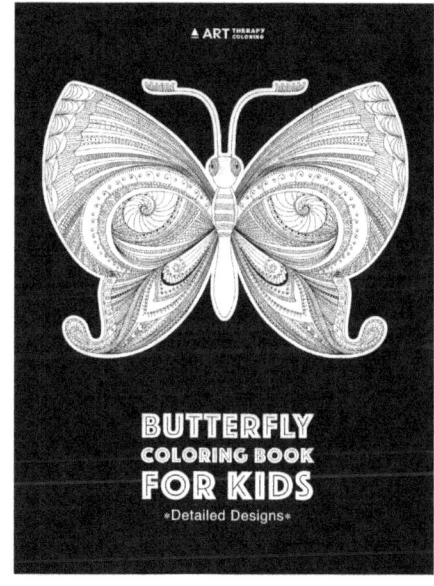

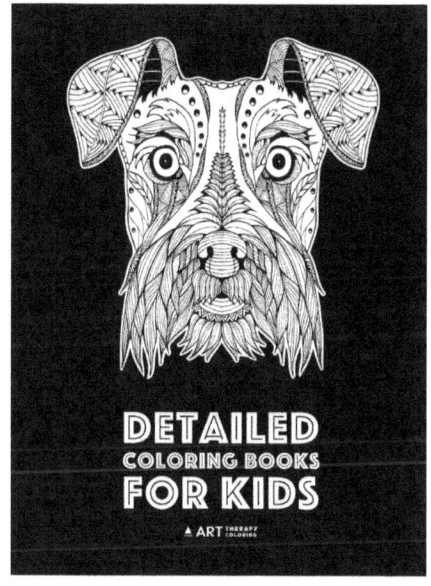

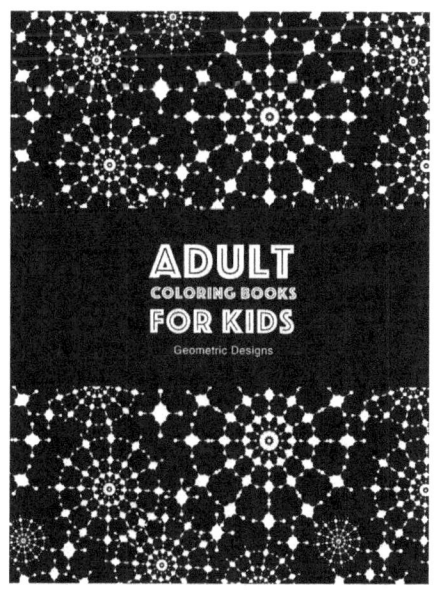

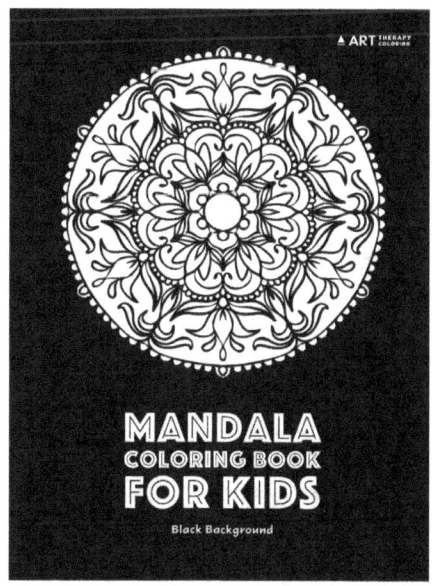

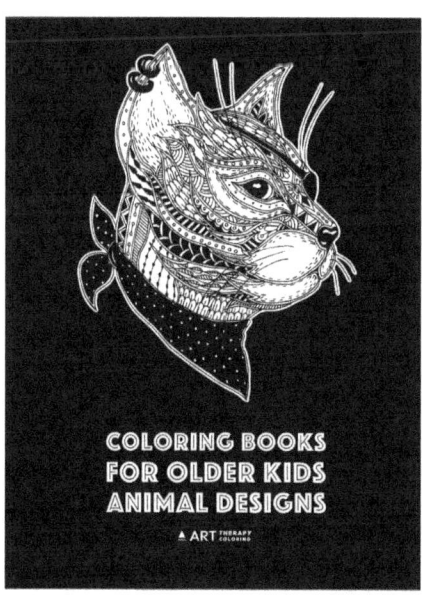

# Coloring Books For Teens

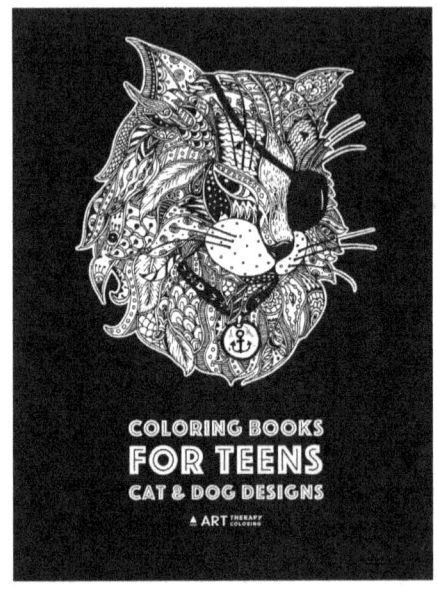

COLORING BOOKS
**FOR TEENS**
CAT & DOG DESIGNS
ART THERAPY COLORING

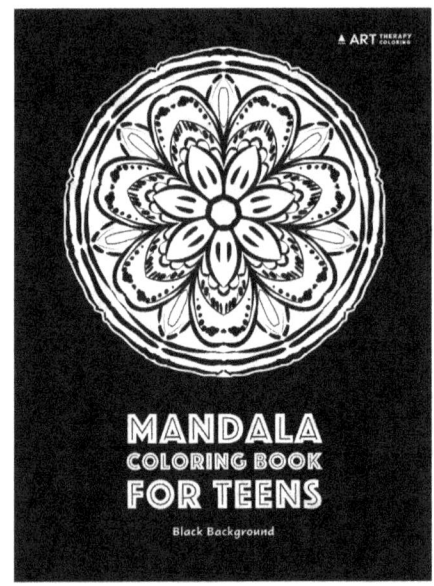

**MANDALA**
COLORING BOOK
**FOR TEENS**
Black Background

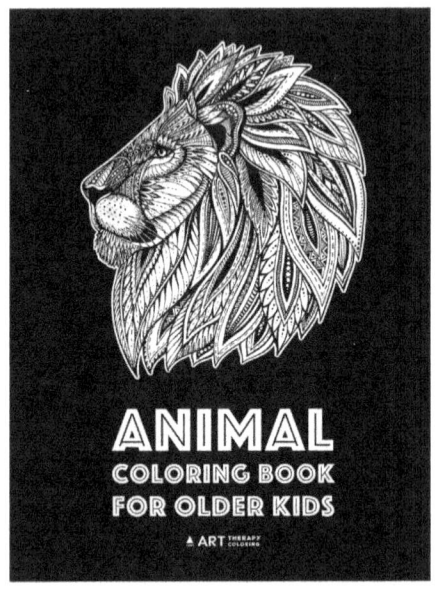

**ANIMAL**
COLORING BOOK
FOR OLDER KIDS
ART THERAPY COLORING

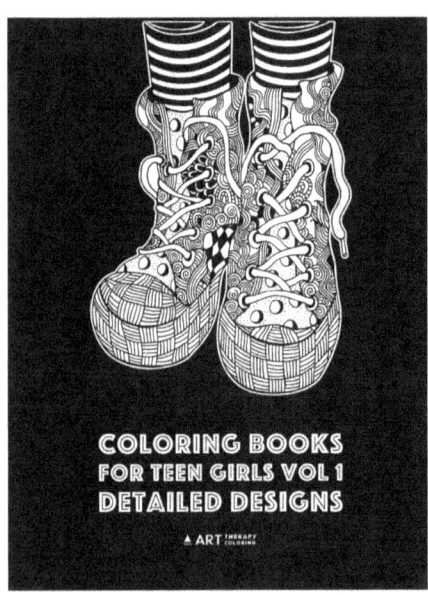

COLORING BOOKS
FOR TEEN GIRLS VOL 1
DETAILED DESIGNS
ART THERAPY COLORING

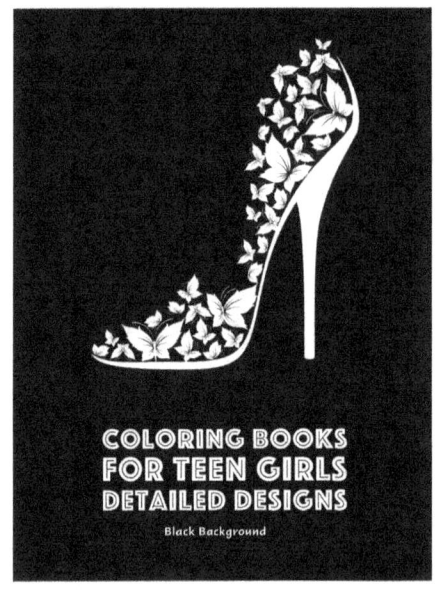

COLORING BOOKS
FOR TEEN GIRLS
DETAILED DESIGNS
Black Background

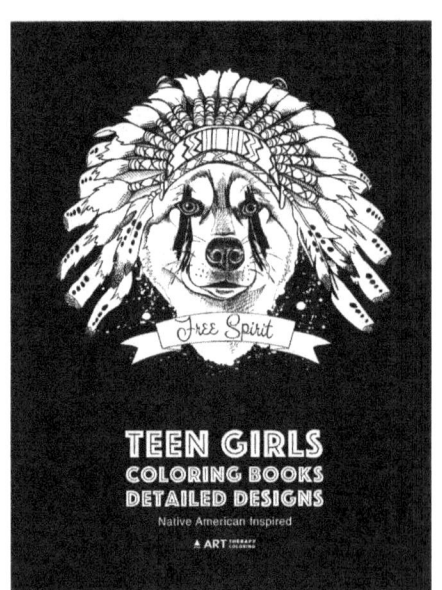

Free Spirit

TEEN GIRLS
COLORING BOOKS
DETAILED DESIGNS
Native American Inspired
ART THERAPY COLORING

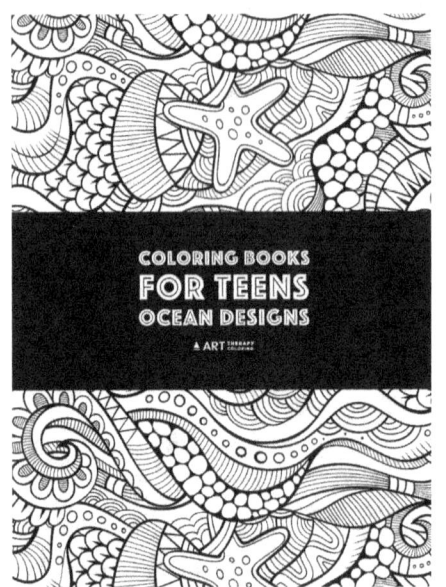

COLORING BOOKS
**FOR TEENS**
OCEAN DESIGNS
ART THERAPY COLORING

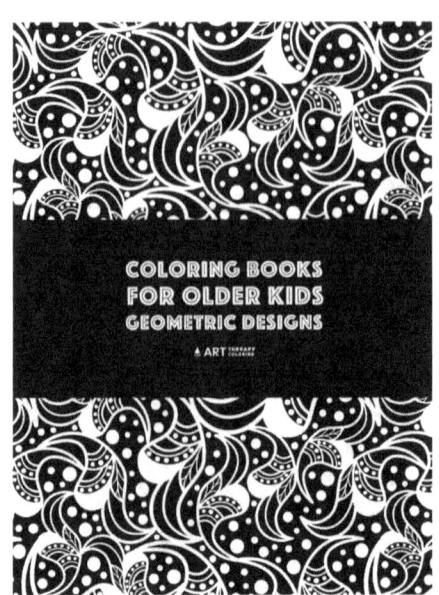

COLORING BOOKS
FOR OLDER KIDS
GEOMETRIC DESIGNS
ART THERAPY COLORING

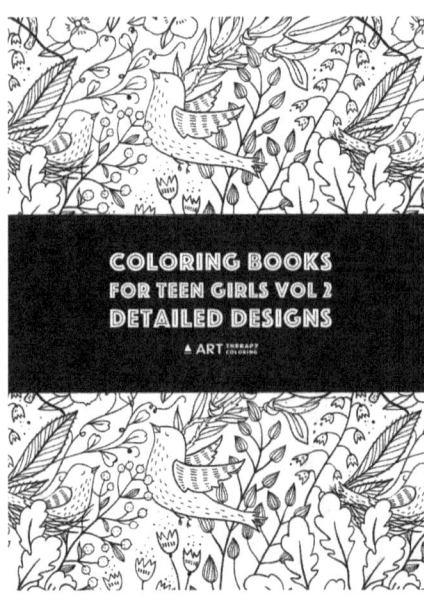

COLORING BOOKS
FOR TEEN GIRLS VOL 2
DETAILED DESIGNS
ART THERAPY COLORING

# Coloring Books For Teens

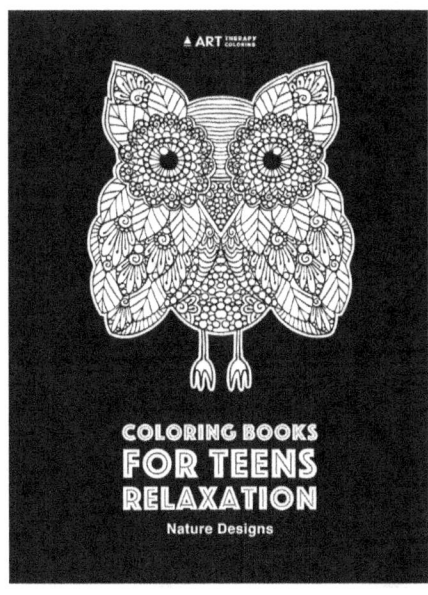

COLORING BOOKS
**FOR TEENS
RELAXATION**
Nature Designs

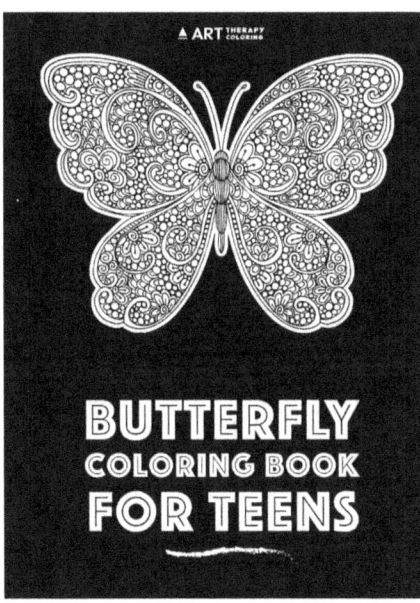

**BUTTERFLY**
COLORING BOOK
**FOR TEENS**

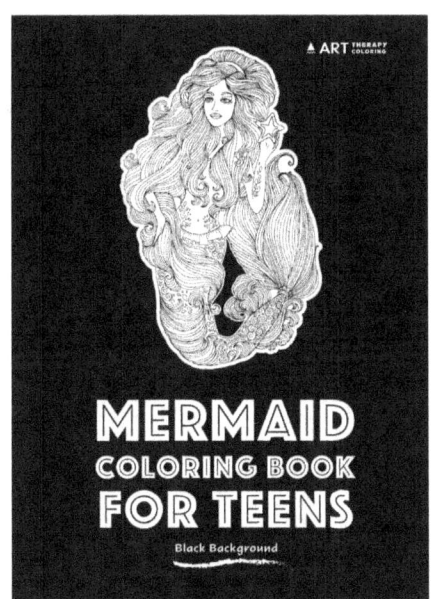

**MERMAID**
COLORING BOOK
**FOR TEENS**
Black Background

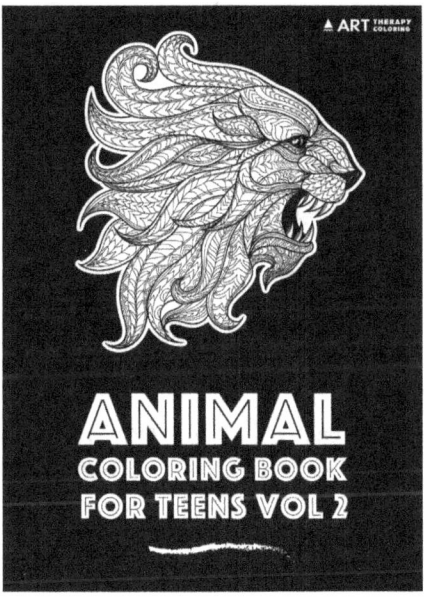

**ANIMAL**
COLORING BOOK
**FOR TEENS VOL 2**

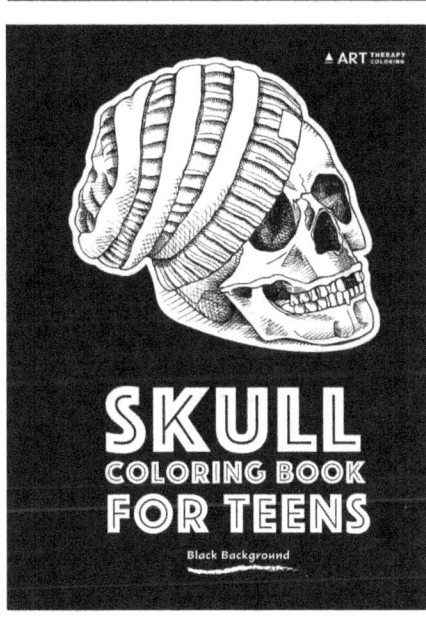

**SKULL**
COLORING BOOK
**FOR TEENS**
Black Background

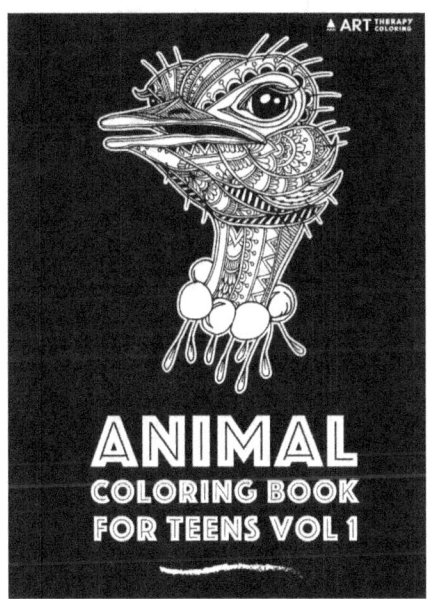

**ANIMAL**
COLORING BOOK
**FOR TEENS VOL 1**

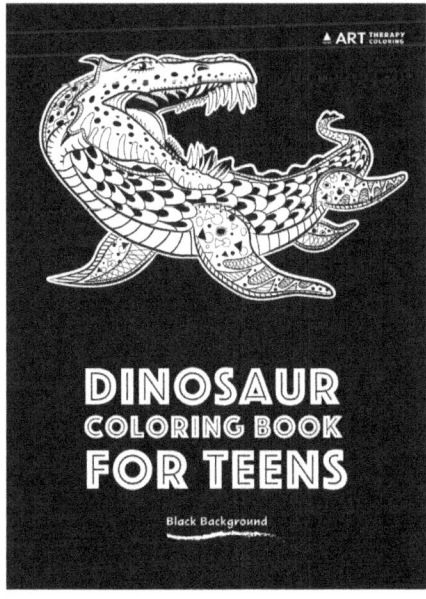

**DINOSAUR**
COLORING BOOK
**FOR TEENS**
Black Background

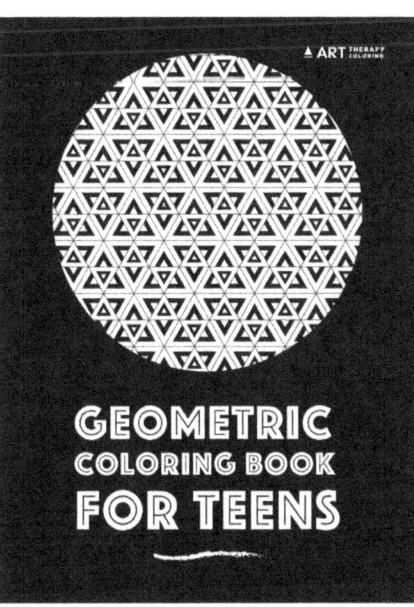

**GEOMETRIC**
COLORING BOOK
**FOR TEENS**

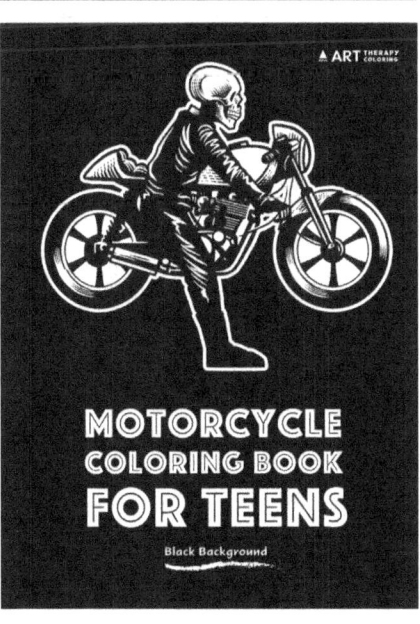

**MOTORCYCLE**
COLORING BOOK
**FOR TEENS**
Black Background

# Coloring Books For Teens

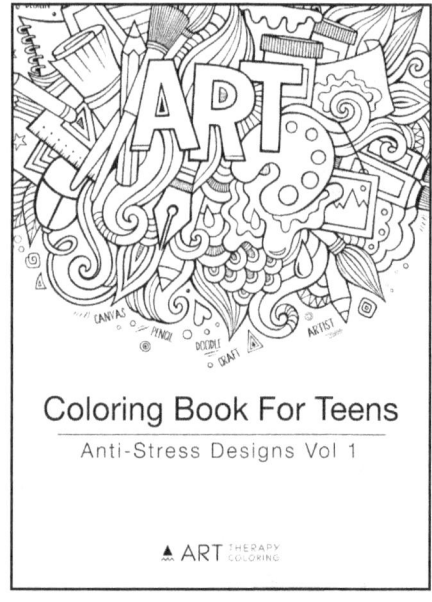

## Coloring Book For Teens
Anti-Stress Designs Vol 1

▲ ART THERAPY COLORING

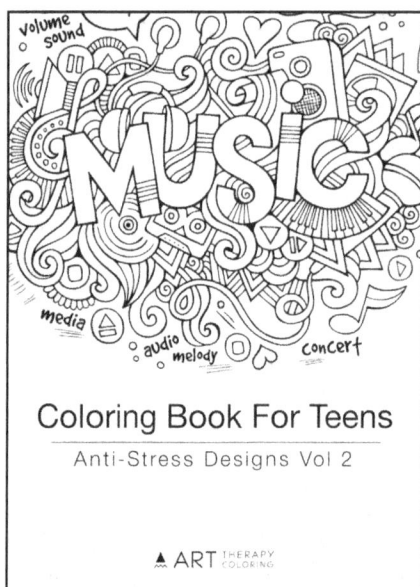

## Coloring Book For Teens
Anti-Stress Designs Vol 2

▲ ART THERAPY COLORING

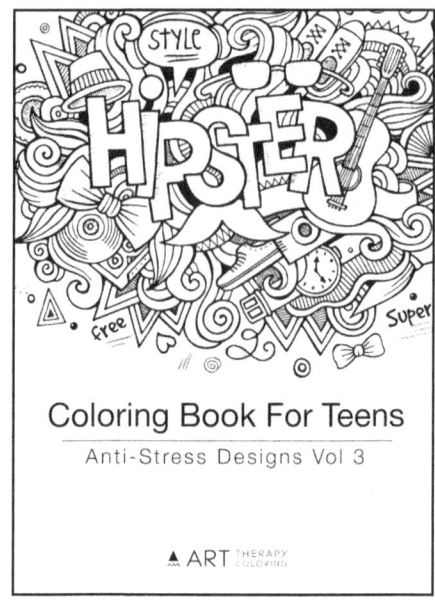

## Coloring Book For Teens
Anti-Stress Designs Vol 3

▲ ART THERAPY COLORING

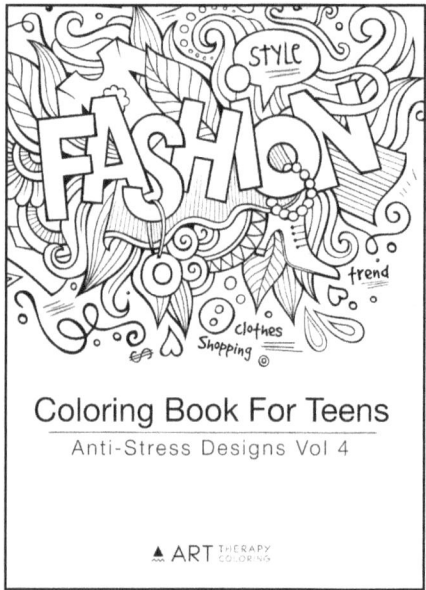

## Coloring Book For Teens
Anti-Stress Designs Vol 4

▲ ART THERAPY COLORING

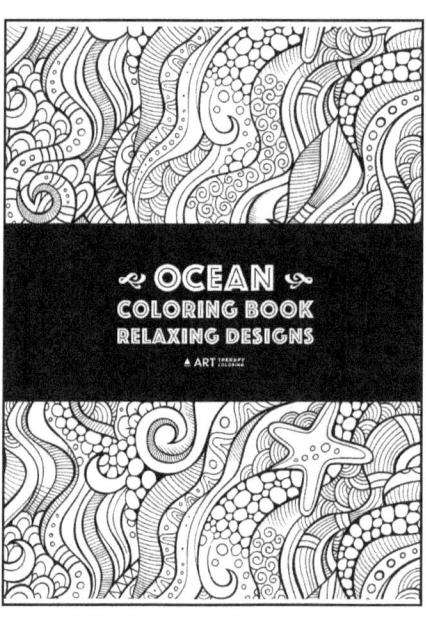

OCEAN COLORING BOOK RELAXING DESIGNS
▲ ART THERAPY COLORING

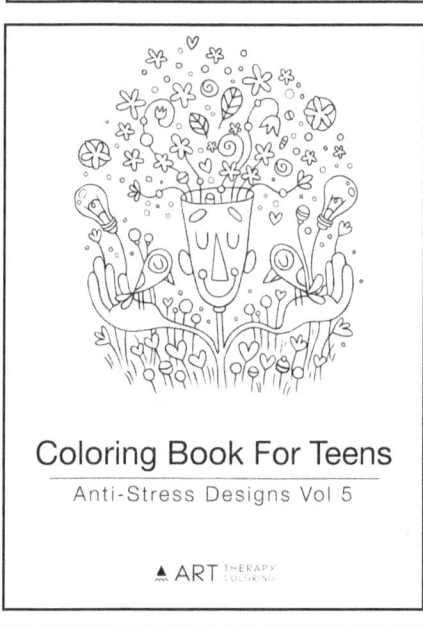

## Coloring Book For Teens
Anti-Stress Designs Vol 5

▲ ART THERAPY COLORING

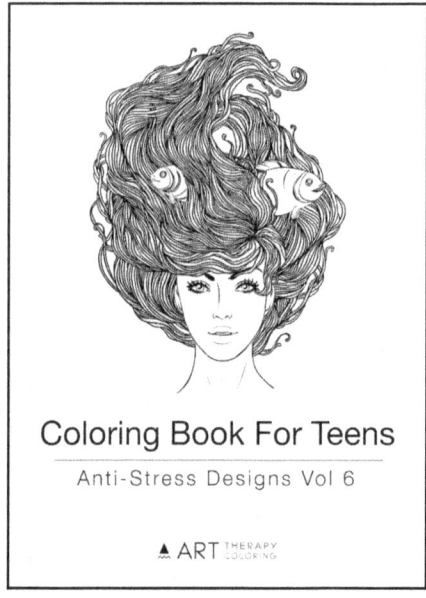

## Coloring Book For Teens
Anti-Stress Designs Vol 6

▲ ART THERAPY COLORING

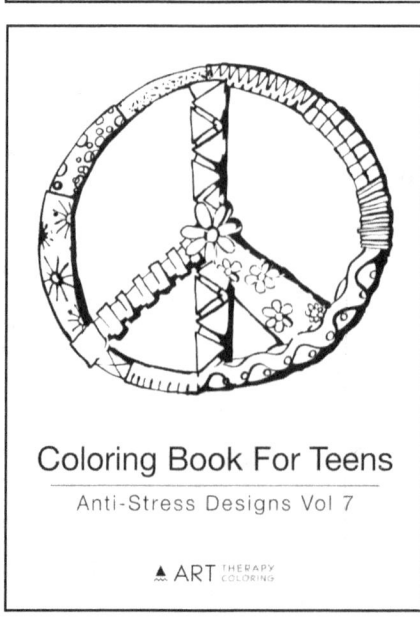

## Coloring Book For Teens
Anti-Stress Designs Vol 7

▲ ART THERAPY COLORING

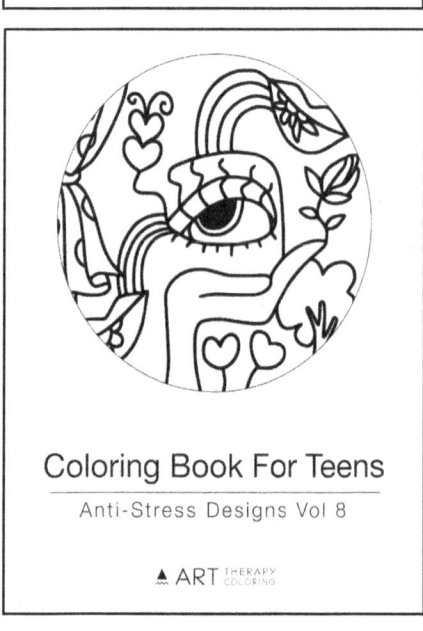

## Coloring Book For Teens
Anti-Stress Designs Vol 8

▲ ART THERAPY COLORING

# Coloring Books For Special Occasions

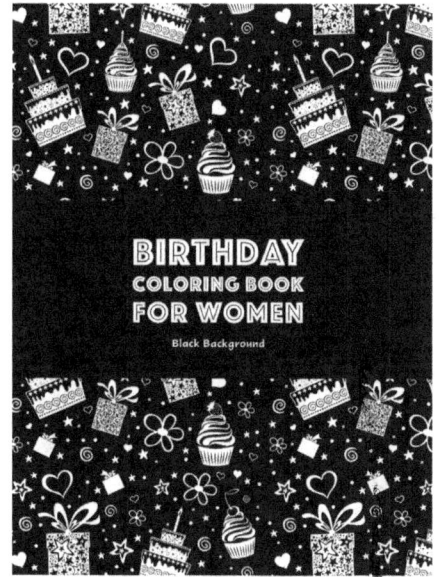

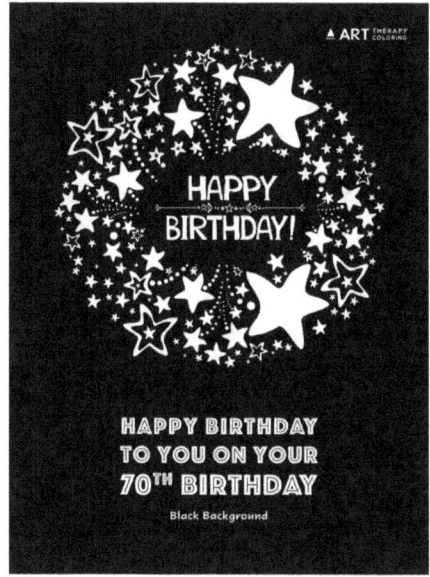

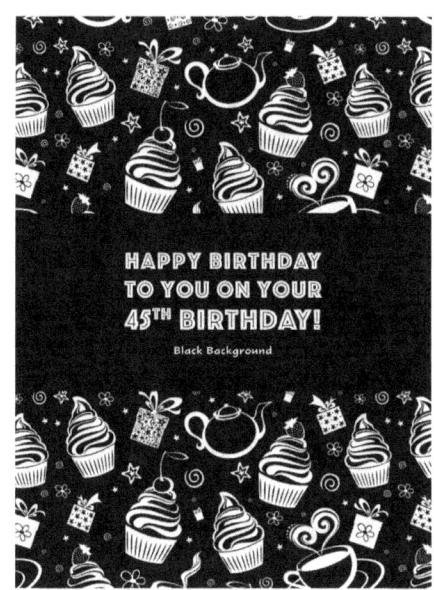

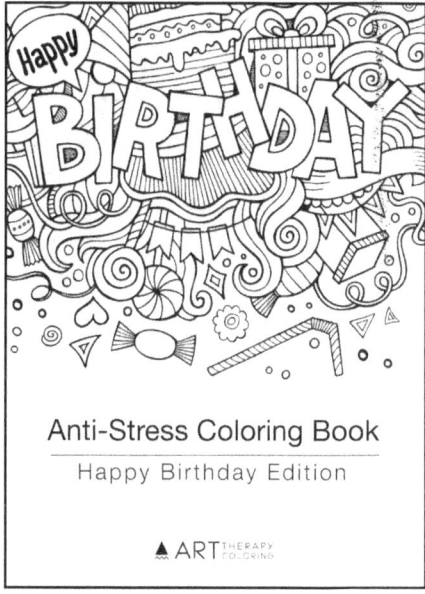

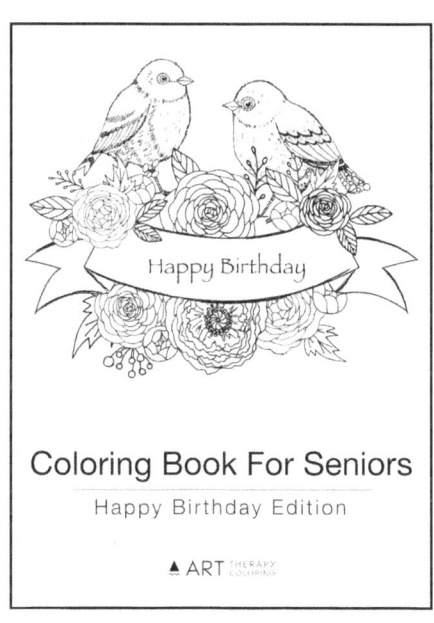

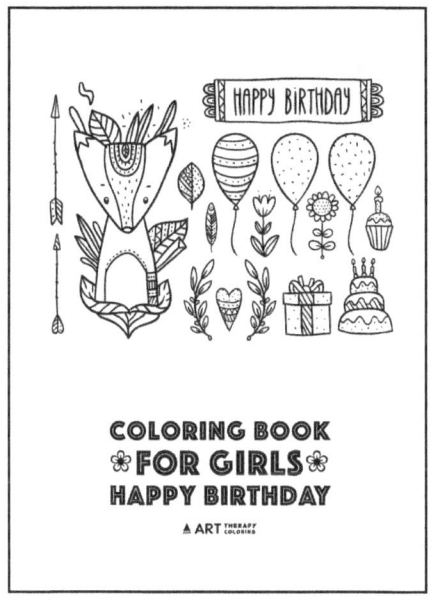

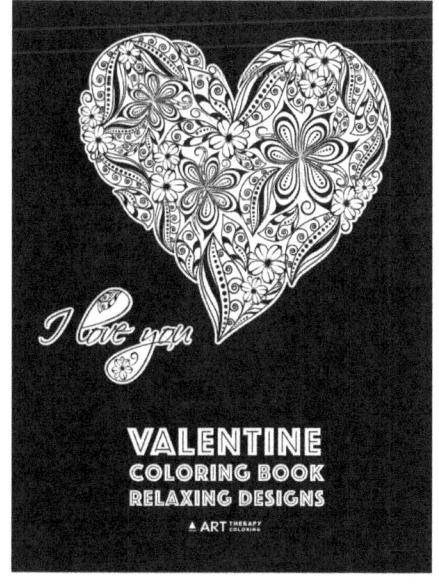

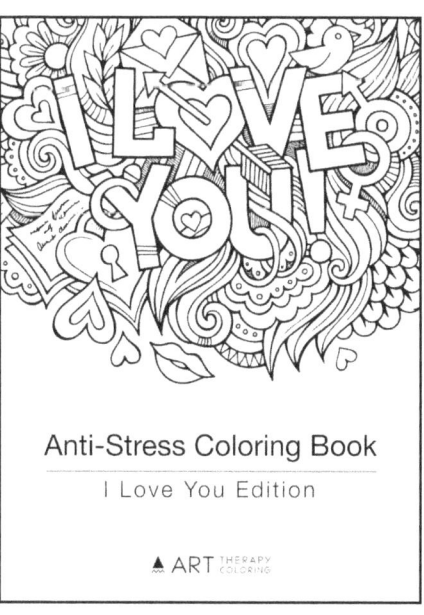

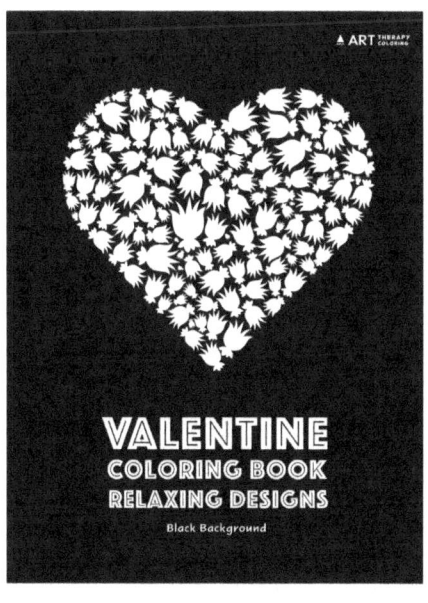

# Coloring Books For Christmas

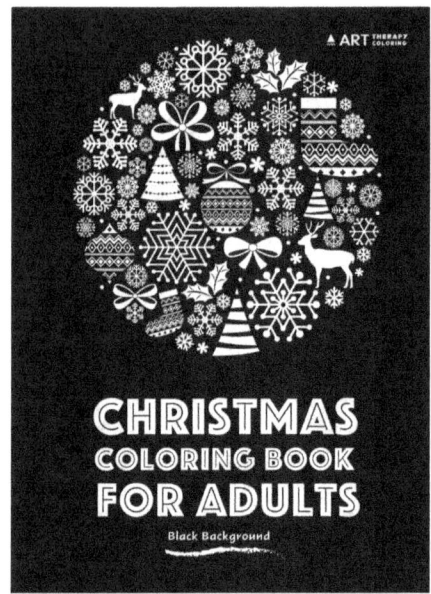

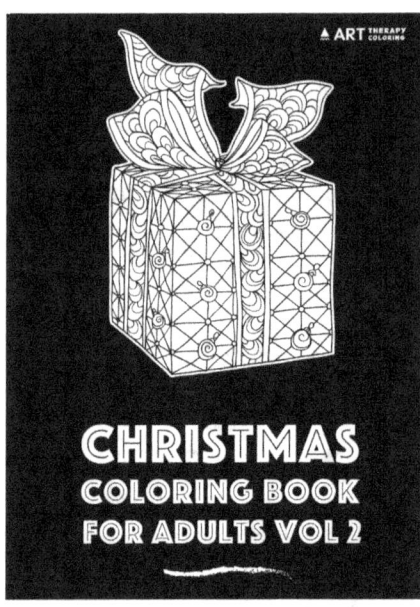

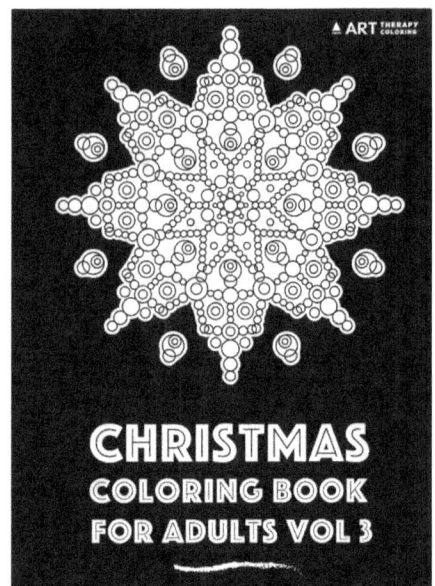

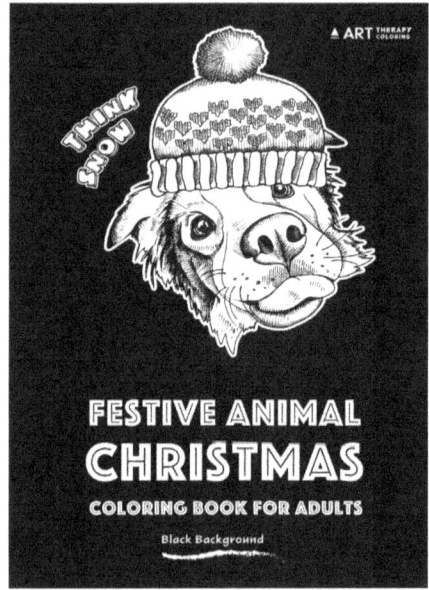

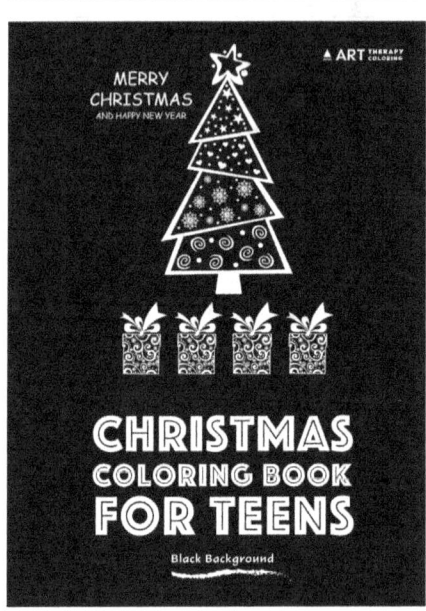

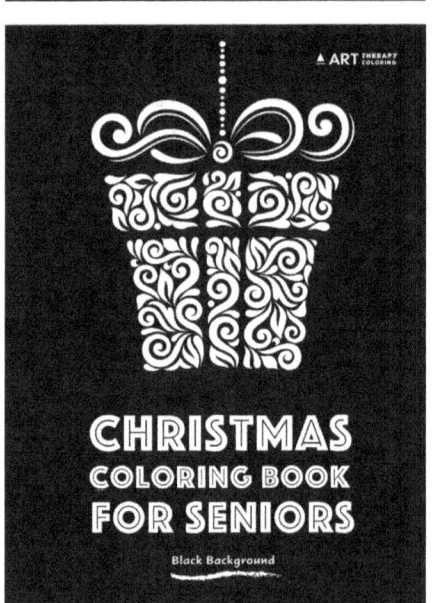

Swirls Coloring Book
Relaxing Designs

Published by:
Art Therapy Coloring
El Dorado Hills, California
www.arttherapycoloring.com

Shutterstock Images

ISBN: 978-1-64126-065-7